Make a Joyful Noise unto the Lord!

The Life of Mahalia Jackson, Queen of Gospel Singers

WOMEN OF AMERICA
Milton Meltzer, Editor

Make a Joyful Noise unto the Lord!

The Life of Mahalia Jackson, Queen of Gospel Singers

JESSE JACKSON

Illustrated with Photographs

THOMAS Y. CROWELL COMPANY   NEW YORK

Picture Editor: R. Lynn Goldberg
Designed by Angela Foote
Manufactured in the United States of America

Library of Congress Cataloging in Publication Data

Jackson, Jesse.
Make a joyful noise unto the Lord!

(Women of America)
SUMMARY: A biography of the famous black gospel
singer who hoped, through her art, to break down
some of the barriers between black and white people.
Bibliography: p.
1. Jackson, Mahalia, 1911–1972—Juv. lit.
[1. Jackson, Mahalia, 1911–1972. 2. Singers—United
States] I. Title.
ML3930.J2J2   783′.7[B] [92]   72–7549
ISBN 0–690–43344–1

ISBN 0–690–43344–1

10   9   8   7   6   5   4   3

This book is for Ann and Judith

ACKNOWLEDGMENTS

We wish to thank the late Mahalia Jackson for her help. She was a great singer and a superb talker. As conductor of her own television show, as a guest artist on countless radio and television programs, and as the subject of hundreds of newspaper and magazine features, she sang the songs she had to sing the way she wanted to sing them and said what she had to say without biting her tongue. The author regrets not having space for more of the wonderful things Mahalia said about her life, her music, the black experience, religion, and God.

Thanks are due to Mrs. Jane Brightman Dunne for digging up many of Mahalia's statements; to Studs Terkel for giving us hours of taped interviews with Mahalia on Chicago's station WFMT; to James B. Poteat of the Television Information Office (National Association of Broadcasters) for his assistance; to Omer Persons of Columbia Records for the listing of the gospel singer's records and information about them; and to Joe Bostic, one of Mahalia's earliest promoters. Our thanks also to Benjamin L. Hooks, Federal Communications Commissioner, an old friend and lawyer for Mahalia; and to Sally Martin, who recalled for us the old days when Mahalia sang for nickels, dimes, and collar buttons. We are grateful to one of the Reverend Martin Luther King's attorneys (who did not wish to be named) for valuable information about the moral and financial support the singer gave the martyr. And many thanks to the book's editors—Milton Meltzer, without whose help this work would not have seen the light of day, and Matilda Welter, for whose patience in seeing the book through the author has the deepest respect. Whatever errors remain in it belong to the writer.

Here are some of the published items the author drew on:

SONGBOOKS

> Dorsey, Thomas A. *Great Gospel Songs*. New York: Hill and Range Songs, Inc., 1965.
> Sandburg, Carl. *The American Songbag*. New York: Harcourt, Brace, 1927.

Work, John W., and Work, Frederick J. *Folk Songs of the American Negro*. Nashville: Work Brothers, 1901.

BOOKS ABOUT JAZZ

Blesh, Rudi. *Shining Trumpets, A History of Jazz*. New York: Alfred A. Knopf, 1946.

Erlich, Lillian. *What Jazz Is All About*. New York: Julian Messner, 1962.

Feather, Leonard. *The Encyclopedia of Jazz*. New York: Horizon, 1960.

Goldberg, Joe. *Jazz Masters of the Fifties*. New York: Macmillan, 1965.

Hughes, Langston. *Famous Negro Music Makers*. New York: Dodd, Mead, 1955.

————. *The First Book of Jazz*. New York: Franklin Watts, 1954.

Jones, Le Roi. *Blues People*. New York: Morrow, 1963.

Montgomery, Elizabeth Rider. *The Story Behind Popular Songs*. New York: Dodd, Mead, 1961.

Morris, Berenice Robinson. *American Popular Music: The Beginning Years*. New York: Franklin Watts, 1970.

Posell, Elsa Z. *American Composers*. Boston: Houghton, Mifflin, 1963.

Rublowsky, John. *Music in America*. New York: Crowell-Collier, 1967.

Stearns, Marshall. *The Story of Jazz*. New York: Oxford, 1956.

INDIVIDUAL BIOGRAPHIES

Anderson, Marian. *My Lord, What a Morning: An Autobiography*. New York: Viking, 1956.

Graham, Shirley. *Paul Robeson, Citizen of the World*. New York: Julian Messner, 1946, 1971.

Helm, MacKinley. *Angel Mo' and Her Son, Roland Hayes*. Boston: Little, Brown, 1942.

Jackson, Mahalia, and Wylie, Evan M. *Movin' on Up*. New York: Hawthorn, 1966.

BOOKS ABOUT BLACK HISTORY

Hansberry, Lorraine. *The Movement: Documentary of a Struggle For Equality*. New York: Simon & Schuster, 1964.

Hughes, Langston, and Meltzer, Milton. *Black Magic: A Pictorial History of the Negro in American Entertainment*. New York: Crown, 1967.

————. *A Pictorial History of the Negro in America*. New York: Crown, 1968.

Contents

Make a Joyful Noise unto the Lord!

The Life of Mahalia Jackson, Queen of Gospel Singers

•❧ *1* ❧•

Little Girl with a Big Voice

Mahalia was the third of six Jackson children, all of them born in the same shack with a leaky roof on Water Street. That's in New Orleans, the big town at the foot of the Mississippi, where the great river pours into the Gulf of Mexico.

At the time Mahalia was born—it was October 26, 1911—one side of Water Street was walled in by a levee high enough to keep the rampaging Mississippi floods back, if they didn't rise *too* high. On the other side were the railroad trains, spouting their steam and smoke across the roofs of the unpainted hovels, the shops selling molasses, cornmeal, and meat (the three *m's* blacks had lived on since slavery times), and the tiny storefront

1

churches where blacks went to sing and give thanks for being alive.

Living in that slum between the levee and the tracks was hard. Water Street was unpaved; it was dusty during dry spells and when it rained, you had to walk ankle-deep in mud. All the water for household use came from a common pump at one end of the street. Before anyone drank it, the mud had to be filtered from it with cornmeal —if cornmeal could be spared. And even then the water had to be boiled to kill the fatal typhoid germs.

Mahalia's mother, Charity, was one of the Clark family. The Clarks had lived for generations on the Gumpstump cotton plantation, deep in Louisiana's backwoods, north of New Orleans. Before the Civil War, they had all been slaves. When the war ended and Emancipation came, they became sharecroppers. Life turned into another form of slavery, called peonage. They worked twelve hours a day, sunup to sundown, and got seventy-five cents for it. They rarely saw the money. It went down on the books in the planter's store, the same books where he kept account of the supplies he sold them. With the high prices he charged and the way he kept his books, the blacks always ended the year in debt.

It was Charity's brother, whom Mahalia called Uncle Porter, who rescued the Clarks from the plantation. He had risen from a dishwasher on a riverboat to dining-car chef on a luxury train. He brought his father and sisters —Charity, Duke, Bessie, Alice, Hannah, and Belle—to Water Street. Charity was a pretty brown woman, frail but high-spirited. She was Uncle Porter's favorite and beloved by all her sisters.

It was on Water Street that Charity Clark met and married John Jackson. Mahalia's father was a light-skinned, sad-faced man, doomed all his life to dream of better times. Not that he didn't have energy. He had to have it to support Charity and his six children. He unloaded ships during the day, barbered in a makeshift shop in the evening, and preached the gospel according to the Holiness creed on Sundays.

Kerosene lamps lit the Jackson home at night; an iron stove warmed them in winter. Charity cooked the family's food on the stove in all seasons, using driftwood washed up by the Mississippi or coal from the railroad tracks for fuel. What Mahalia's home lacked in comforts was made up for by the love of her parents and of her aunts and uncles. And by music.

Mahalia learned early to love sound and song. There were red and green songbirds on the river. Woodpeckers kept the beat. Crickets piped the choruses. Street peddlers sang about their wares: "Deviled crabs! Blackberries! Fresh and fine! Boiled shrimps!" She heard sailors' work songs. She fell asleep to the tunes made by river boats tooting and trains whistling those been-here-and-gone blues in the sad night.

One lively song Mahalia loved especially—the Mardi Gras song. As the time for the annual New Orleans Mardi Gras Carnival approached, Mahalia would hear Water Street's black musicians, the ones who were members of the Zulu Aid and Pleasure Marching Club, practicing it. And it wasn't long before she learned the words:

> *If ever I cease to love,*
> *If ever I cease to love,*
> *May the fish get legs*
> *And the cows lay eggs—*
> *If ever I cease to love!*

At other times, especially when she sat with her mother in Mount Moriah Baptist Church on Sundays, Mahalia sang church songs. Mardi Gras music and church music—they weren't the same thing. Not to churchgoers. They said you had to make a choice between them. It was like choosing between the devil and God. You couldn't have it both ways.

Mahalia liked them both. She was too young to know any difference. By the time she was four, she had her heart set on singing in the Baptist choir. In her father's Holiness church the little girl was caught up by the beat of tambourines the worshipers shook to guide them through their soaring songs. The Holiness people shouted during service; their bodies swayed with the rhythm; they stamped their feet when God told them to and clapped their hands when He spoke to them. It was different in the Baptist church, where tambourines were forbidden. There they sang sweet; yes, it was beautiful, but it wasn't the jubilation sound of the Holiness people.

Little Mahalia began to clap her hands the way the others did. When she heard the singers cry out for God's protection and tap their feet, she tapped hers. Gradually she learned the simply worded songs.

Charity tried to explain to Mahalia the difference between a Mardi Gras song and a church song. Unsaved, frivolous and downright bad people seeking pleasure in this world, sang Mardi Gras songs, Charity said. Saved, serious people seeking to make a better world and prepare themselves for God's heaven sang church songs. Especially Baptist songs.

Mahalia made up her mind not to sing Mardi Gras songs. She wanted so badly to sing in the Baptist choir! But first, Charity explained, she'd have to join the Baptist church.

What must she do to become a member?

She would have to ask to sit on the mourners' bench. While she sat there, members of the church would pray that God might save, protect, and welcome her into the church. Then, after that, she would have to confess her sins, be baptized, and be born again as though she had risen from the dead.

In time Mahalia did all these things. Now she was ready to try out for the choir. But how was she to learn what to sing? Not from any printed music. There were no songbooks in the tiny church. Besides, few members could read. The songs they sang, the words and the music, had passed down from one generation of blacks to the next, learned and remembered with pride. The old slave codes had made it illegal for blacks to be taught to read and write. Perhaps, if the songs had been written down, some of their magic and spirit would have been lost. Spirituals, they were called, and rightly so, because they rose from the need to bolster spirits in the long dark days of slavery.

So before Mahalia was five, she learned the remembered songs, the songs that rose from the spirit, from the need and suffering of her people. One day Charity said, "Little Haley's ready."

At the tryout for the choir, Mahalia waited her turn. Then she opened her mouth and began: "I'm so glad, I'm so glad, / I'm so glad I've been in the grave an' rose again. . . ."

People passing outside the Water Street church stopped to listen to a new sound.

When she finished, there was admiring silence. From then on, until the day she left New Orleans, people would speak of her as "the little girl with the big voice."

She had become a member of Mount Moriah's choir.

⤳ 2 ⤳

"Been in the Grave an' Rose Again"

What was there to sing about? When you were black and in New Orleans? "If I owned a home in hell and one in New Orleans, I'd rent out the one in New Orleans and live in hell." Blacks laughed when they said this. But it was laughing to keep from crying. New Orleans—the whole South—had a long history of discrimination. When Mahalia's mother or father took her someplace too far to walk, they rode in a streetcar for blacks only. Twenty-one years before Mahalia was born, Louisiana had adopted a law requiring railroads to carry black passengers in separate cars (called "Jim Crow" cars) or behind partitions.

Early in the 1890's, a young New Orleans black, Homer Plessy, had decided to challenge that law. He bought a ticket in New Orleans for Covington, Louisiana, got on the train, and took a seat in the "white" car. The conductor ordered him to move to the Jim Crow car. He refused. The police came and arrested him. At the trial, Plessy's lawyer argued before Judge John B. Ferguson that the Jim Crow law was unconstitutional. It violated the Fourteenth Amendment to the Constitution, which said no state could make a law depriving a citizen of his equal rights. Judge Ferguson ruled against Plessy. He declared him guilty of breaking the separate car law.

Plessy wouldn't accept Jim Crow. He fought the case up to the United States Supreme Court. In 1896 the Court's majority decided against Plessy. Segregation didn't discriminate against Negroes, they said, ignoring the fact that white Southerners all along had boasted that the sole reason for the Jim Crow laws was to degrade blacks. The Court said a state did have the right to label its citizens by their race, providing there were "separate but equal" public facilities for blacks.

Jim Crow was now made legal and official. It was the green light for Southern communities, and some places in the North, too, to pile on Jim Crow laws. Signs saying WHITE ONLY or COLORED popped up everywhere. Water bubblers, toilets, waiting rooms, ticket windows, all were tagged by race to keep whites and blacks from meeting on equal terms.

Whatever Mahalia did when she was growing up in New Orleans, wherever she went, Jim Crow ruled—except on Water Street. Her own neighborhood was mixed. French, Italians, Creoles lived side by side with the blacks, all of them sweating hard to make ends meet. And the children played together, sharing fun one minute and fighting the next. But being black when they were that little made no difference on Water Street, Mahalia said.

Everywhere else, it did make a difference. She couldn't go to the same school with white children. Their schoolbooks couldn't even be stored in the same warehouse. She couldn't go to the circus with whites. The circus set aside one day for blacks to watch the clowns. Blacks couldn't attend white churches. During a court trial they couldn't even take an oath on the same Bible. The law required there be one Bible for blacks to swear to tell the truth, the whole truth, and nothing but the truth, and one for whites to swear on. If her father wanted to go fishing with a white friend, they couldn't lunch together in a normal way. The law made them put an oar across the middle of the boat and sit with the oar between them while they ate.

Black friends couldn't even talk together without fear that a white policeman would suspect they were plotting something. Everyone in New Orleans knew about the time when young Leonard Pierce and Robert Charles were sitting on a stoop on Dryades Street, close by Water Street. Three police officers walked up with guns out and without cause or warrant tried to arrest them. Pierce submitted, but Charles wouldn't. He knew what the odds were against a black getting a fair trial in the white man's court. He resisted. Shots were fired and drew blood on both sides. Charles fled, and a citywide manhunt was on. Mobs raced through the streets, hunting down blacks. Three were killed before the police found out where Charles was hiding. From the besieged house he defended himself with a rifle. The police set fire to the house, and when Charles was forced to run out, the mob caught him and lynched him.

Robert Charles, "the baddest black New Orleans had ever seen," wasn't all that people talked about. Mahalia and her brother Peter sometimes strayed from Water Street and wandered downtown to Baronne, Saratoga, and Ramparts streets. They'd end up in Beauregard Square, once known as the Place Congo. They'd heard the folks in Water Street talk about Congo Square and how the slaves used to go there on Sunday afternoons and church holy days to make music and dance under the vigilant eye of the police. A few thousand people would gather to watch the five or six hundred dancers, assembled in groups in different parts of the square. Each group had its own orchestra—drums, rattles, and stringed instruments made by themselves. They would form in rings and dance a kind of shuffle step, beginning slowly and building up to wild, frenzied movements. Chants accompanied the instruments, lasting as long as five or six hours.

New Orleans was the most musical city in the land in Mahalia's early years. Besides the annual Mardi Gras and the Sundays in the Place Congo, there were operas and concerts in which highly trained black musicians performed. For years, the emotional and powerfully rhythmic African music of the slaves had stood in sharp contrast to the European music of the cultured free blacks. By Mahalia's time, the two traditions were merged. And out of them had come a new music with new sounds, a modern music that voiced the life of the twentieth century.

Soon after Mahalia joined Mount Moriah's choir, her mother fell sick. No one, not even the doctor, knew what the trouble was. If God saw fit to take her, Charity worried, what would become of the children? She hoped her sisters would not let her husband's cousins take Mahalia. They were part of Ma Rainey's Rabbit Foot Minstrels. Ma was a blues singer who toured around the South. Charity didn't want her Mahalia traipsing around in a minstrel show.

One day, a few months later, Mahalia came in from playing on the street to find that her mother had died. She watched the neighbors bring in covered pots and dishes of cooked pig's feet, baked alligator tail, black-eyed beans and rice, corn bread, and chitterlings.

The women from the Holiness church, where her father preached on Sundays, and from her mother's Baptist burial society disagreed over which church Charity's funeral should be held in. The women from the burial society stood pat. They held the money to pay the undertaker. A burial society pooled the pennies of church members into a fund that assured the dead a decent burial and some help for their survivors. The Holiness people, on the other hand, were sure their leader, John Jackson, would have his way in the burial of his wife.

Aunt Duke stepped in between the Baptists and the Holiness partisans. She was a powerfully built woman with dark brown skin and gray eyes. She carried herself erect as a drum major. She was a no-nonsense Baptist. Everything that wasn't honest work and steady church attendance, she looked upon as sin. Blacks who played jazz or sang the blues—well, they were unsaved and beyond redemption.

Aunt Duke ruled that the burial society should take charge of Charity's funeral. But in which church? And when? Before Charity died, she had asked Aunt Duke to promise her that the funeral would be held in old St. John's Baptist Church and that she would be buried in its graveyard on the Gumpstump plantation.

But Mahalia's father was against having the funeral in a Baptist church. What would the congregation of his church think if he did not have his wife's funeral in the Holiness church? Aunt Duke suggested the question remain undecided till Uncle Porter got there.

When Uncle Porter arrived, he said that Charity was his favorite sister. He wanted her wishes carried out to the letter. First she should have her funeral in Mount Moriah Baptist Church. And that would get her prepared for final burial in St. John's Church out at Gumpstump plantation. Mr. Jackson's heart sank. The funeral date was set, and the last night of the wake began.

The sound of the wake, an all-night vigil attended by members of Charity's church, the burial society, her neighbors and next of kin, filled the house. So there was no need to fear that evil spirits might harm Charity or steal her soul—which is the reason why wakes were held originally.

When Mahalia woke on the day of the funeral, familiar sounds seemed changed. Were the trains next to Water Street running more slowly? The Mississippi, on the other side of Water Street, lay quiet. The birds were silent.

Mahalia had cried her eyes out. There were no tears left when she entered Mount Moriah Baptist Church. But as someone began moaning the refrain of "Mother's Gone On to Prepare a Place for Us," she wept anew.

After the singing ended and the preacher finished his sermon, the family went up for a last look at Charity. Aunt Duke held Mahalia in her arms so the child could see her mother. Then they put the lid on Charity's casket. They took her to the train for the burial at Gumpstump.

When they started back home, Uncle Porter began singing:

I'm so glad, I'm so glad,
I'm so glad I've been in the grave an' rose again. . . .

❧ 3 ❧

"A-Lookin' for a Home"

That night, after her mother's burial, Mahalia went to live at the home of Aunt Duke and her husband, Emanuel Paul. Their house was on Water Street, too. Her other aunts took in four of Mahalia's brothers and sisters. Only Peter, who was five years older than she, remained with Mahalia. Mahalia cried the rest of her tears that night after she went to bed. Aunt Duke was wonderful, but that didn't make up for not being in the same home with all her sisters and brothers. It was something too painful to grasp. She could not understand it. At last she fell asleep.

Later she was awakened by the sound of a phonograph next door. The record it was playing—was it Ma

Rainey's voice? Or was it Bessie Smith singing? Uncle Porter had said that Bessie Smith had learned the blues from Ma Rainey. It was hard for Mahalia to tell one from the other.

After a moment Mahalia decided it was Ma Rainey, singing a story about an insect that destroyed the cotton crop. Mahalia closed her eyes. She wanted to sleep. But the slow contralto voice spelling out the sad story kept her awake:

> De Boll Weevil is a little black bug
> F'um Mexico, dey say.
> He come to try dis Louisiana soil
> An' thought he'd better stay—
> A-lookin' for a home,
> A-lookin' for a home,
> He's a-lookin' for a home.

As she tried to go back to sleep, Mahalia shaped her lips the way she thought the blues singer shaped hers to get the notes to come out right. Finally she fell to dreaming that she was singing with a blues singer in Charity's presence. Mahalia saw her mother shake her head disapprovingly. Church people—the saved—didn't sing the blues. Only sinners—the unsaved—did. In her dreams Mahalia stopped singing. She did not want to offend her mother.

The next morning, after breakfast, Uncle Emanuel took Mahalia's brother Peter off to work with him as yard boy for a white family. He taught Peter how to take care of lawns, shrubbery, and flower gardens. Mahalia began working with Aunt Duke in the garden patch beside their home. The child learned how to weed rows of okra, green beans, red beans, tomatoes, pumpkin, and corn. She learned how to feed the chickens and the goat penned in one corner of the yard, and how to gather fruit in season—the peaches, figs, bananas, oranges—and nuts like pecans, from which Aunt Duke taught her to make pralines, a sugar-nut confection.

When the hot sun made outdoor work too exhausting, Aunt Duke found indoor tasks. Mahalia was a sturdy child. As she grew older, Aunt Duke taught her how to make mattress covers of cement sacks. "Hard work never hurt anyone," Aunt Duke said.

"I'm gonna spit on this hot stove, and if you ain't back by the time the spit dries I'm gonna whup you till you think I'm Robert Charles," her aunt would say when she sent her on an errand.

Aunt Duke wanted to make sure that the little girl with the big voice, who loved music and singing, would know how to work with her hands—as black people had to.

When there was need of furniture, Aunt Duke took Mahalia to a nearby sugarcane plantation. There they collected cane stalks and palm fronds, and wove them into split-bottom cane chairs.

Sometimes Uncle Emanuel took Mahalia and Peter to hunt turtles and alligators in the nearby swamps. Baked alligator tail was great, smothered with onions and garlic and herbs. Now and then Aunt Duke went along with them on fishing trips. When they had caught enough fish, they built a fire, fried the fish, and ate them on the spot.

While Uncle Emanuel was teaching Peter his trade, Aunt Duke began Mahalia's instructions in cooking. Mahalia's course in cooking depended a lot on the can of melted fat that sat on the back of the stove. Into this can went drippings from fried bacon and roast pork. The drippings were used to season collard and mustard greens. They found their way into cornbread and many of Aunt Duke's other masterpieces. Aunt Duke even showed Mahalia how to make soap from the drippings. As they worked together Aunt Duke would hum songs—"Before I'd Be a Slave, I'd Be Buried In My Grave"; "Children, We Shall Be Free"; "Walk Together Children, Don't You Get Weary." Each weekday evening as regular as the ticking of the kitchen clock, Aunt Duke took Mahalia to church for prayer services.

On the way Mahalia always listened to the phonographs playing in the homes on Water Street. She heard Bessie Smith singing W. C. Handy's "St. Louis Blues"— "I hate to see that evenin' sun go down"—and silently moved her lips the way she thought the singer moved hers. "When my baby grows up, she won't sing such songs," Aunt Duke would say, stopping and looking around her in the hope of discovering which one of her erring neighbors was playing the devil's music. "No ma'am," Mahalia would answer, remembering the cat-o'-nine-tails that Aunt Duke sometimes applied to her and her brother's back to punish sin. Unable to tell from where the moaning voice came, Aunt Duke continued on her way, holding Mahalia's hand tightly to keep her safe from hell.

At the prayer meeting, Mahalia would sit beside Aunt Duke and listen to her testify about her troubles, ask forgiveness for her sins, take another hold on her faith, and sing the old songs of hope. While her aunt prayed, Mahalia prayed, too. She knew money was scarce. Already she and Peter were eating their aunt and uncle out of house and home. They had to have shoes and clothing to wear. Things cost a lot these days. Their father didn't have regular work on the docks. He earned little by preaching, and what he got from barbering on Saturdays wasn't enough to feed a cat. And now he had remarried and started another family.

Mahalia knew that Aunt Duke wanted her to get an education. With a little schooling Mahalia could become secretary to the many lodges, burial societies, and church organizations Aunt Duke belonged to. The solution was for Mahalia to work and attend school at the same time.

So after finishing the first grade, she took on a job as well as her schooling. She went to work with her Aunt Belle. Belle was all of twelve, Mahalia seven. Aunt Belle was experienced in taking care of white children and in domestic work. She taught Mahalia all she knew. Working for the Ryder family, Mahalia made the beds, helped the children to dress for school, put away their clothing, served them their breakfast, and washed their dishes. For several years Mahalia took the young Ryders to their school, attended only by whites, then rushed off to her own.

She earned two dollars a week in cash, and got the leftover food and the clothing that the Ryder children had no further use for. Sometimes, when no one saw her, Mahalia hugged a doll belonging to the Ryder girl. She had never owned a doll. Despite the work at home and at the Ryders, and singing in the church choir, Mahalia was an apt student. She quickly learned to read, write, to do sums, and what probably proved most important of all, to figure ways to save money—money with which she planned someday to pay her way to Chicago. Mahalia throve on work. Her body soon caught up with her big voice.

On Saturdays she didn't have to go to school or work at the Ryders. It was a special day for her. After lunch she watched Aunt Duke squint at the kitchen clock. That meant it was time for Mahalia to go to her father's barbershop to ask for money.

"Tell your father you need shoes. You can't go to school barefoot," Aunt Duke said.

On the way to her father's, Mahalia felt Saturday's special flavor in her bones. There was music all along the streets. She stopped to listen to small black boys clicking hollow dried bones, one against another, with a lazy rhythmic beat. She went on and found a man coaxing music by blowing across the mouth of an empty glass gallon jug. A companion brushed an iron nail against the corrugated face of a washboard. The leader of this washboard band, for that's what Water Street people called it, played a Jew's harp.

Farther along, Mahalia fell into step with other youngsters behind the Eureka Brass Band, the pride of New Orleans. They led a funeral march to the cemetery.

The burial societies supported the Eureka Band, and the church people forgave them for playing for sinners in dance halls. The sinners didn't like them the less for playing in churches. Sooner or later the brass band followed church members, sinners, backsliders, and unbelievers, the saved and unsaved, to the graveyard and returned blaring "When the Saints Go Marching In."

Mahalia parted company with the Eureka Band and continued on to her father's barbershop. She was in luck. Her father was intent on trimming a customer's beard and did not see her. She sat quietly to feast her eyes on her father's face. Her father was the handsomest man in New Orleans. The only place she could visit her father was on the job. His new wife did not like Mahalia and made her unwelcome in her house.

"How's my little chocolate drop?" asked her father as the customer got out of the chair.

Mahalia smiled. She wanted him to bounce her on his lap the way he used to. But she was too heavy for that now.

"Aunt Duke sent me for shoe money, Papa," said Mahalia, showing him the hole in her shoe.

Her father searched first one pocket and then another without finding any money. Finally he gave her the fifteen cents the customer had paid him. Mahalia thanked him and tightened her fist around the coins.

"Tell Aunt Duke I'll have more for her Sunday," he said.

Mahalia took the long way home. The music she heard was sadder. She hoped her aunt wouldn't scold her for not bringing home enough money for new shoes.

⋖4⋗

After Saturday Comes Sunday's Song

Mahalia was on her way to church one Sunday morning with Aunt Duke, Uncle Emanuel, and her Aunt Hannah from Chicago. Every Sunday for the eleven years she had been living with Aunt Duke and Uncle Emanuel, she had gone with them to church. Sunday had become more and more special to her. Even though she missed the street music—the singers, the Jew's-harp players, the washboard bands, the brass bands, and the street vendors' crying their shrimp, blackberries, and deviled crabs— Mahalia loved singing in Mount Moriah Baptist's choir. It made Sunday special.

This Sunday might be her last one in New Orleans. At sixteen Mahalia towered over older girls. Three years

22

ago, after the eighth grade, she'd quit school, and hired out as a laundress. Ten hours a day at the ironing board. She was both fast (three minutes for a man's shirt) and skillful (embroidered napkins and fancy linen took a lot of doing). Going to work at an early age had given her a maturity that had broadened the range of her rich voice.

Aunt Hannah, who lived in Chicago, was back in New Orleans for a visit. She wanted Mahalia to go back to Chicago with her. Aunt Duke said no. Hannah argued. Chicago wasn't exactly heaven for blacks, but there were opportunities to escape Jim Crow there, she said. But Aunt Duke was dead set against Mahalia going to that wicked city.

"You wanted to be a trained nurse," Hannah told Mahalia. "What chance have you got here where there's not even a hospital for blacks to go to get care, let alone nurses' training? Sure, it's cold in Chicago. You have to work hard just to eat, pay rent, and keep warm. But you have a chance to make something of yourself."

"Aunt Duke depends on me to write letters for her clubs. I have to visit the sick and help them."

"You're not the only black girl in New Orleans who's gone through the eighth grade."

"I don't want to hurt her. I'll ask God to help me persuade her."

"God's sure got His work cut out for Him."

They followed Aunt Duke and Uncle Emanuel into church. Mahalia left them to join the choir seated behind the preacher. She was troubled. She did not want to spoil this peaceful day. But Hannah was returning to Chicago on Monday. Maybe Aunt Duke wouldn't give her the money she had saved—money Mahalia had earned washing white people's clothes, taking care of white people's babies.

Mahalia sat waiting for that moment when a song would begin like a small flame and blaze into holy fire that would sweep away her troubles. She looked at the faces of the cooks, laundresses, nursemaids, young domestic servants like herself, who had been working for white people from the time they started grammar school—young women earning a couple of dollars a week, cast-off clothing, and leftover food. They'd work for white people till they married and then they'd have to go on working harder to help feed their own families when they weren't making additions to it. They'd have no choice save being some white folks' nigger till they became toothless grannies—too old to leave New Orleans for another chance at a new life.

"Dear God, I want a chance. I've tried to make Aunt Duke understand. I'm willing to work hard to become a nurse. I want to go North and succeed," Mahalia whispered.

She sat there, waiting for an older woman to select a song. Even though Mahalia had sung in the choir for eleven years, the older singers would think her bad-mannered if she led. So Aunt Duke had warned her. Some of the members even said young Mahalia was putting too many frills on the spirituals. Mahalia had to be careful. She had to wait for the song and for God's help. She didn't want to leave New Orleans in disgrace.

A moment passed. Then a song took shape out of the empty air, faint, rhythmic, melodic. It was as though a single pent-up sigh had escaped from the congregation, as though they had momentarily forgotten their own suffering, the suffering of their brothers and sisters.

God's presence was building in the song. Mahalia caught the direction of it. A lump came into her throat. She tried to swallow, and forgetful of Aunt Duke's warning, she threw back her head and raised her hands with their calloused palms outstretched. She whispered the song's first phrase: "Sometimes I feel like a motherless chile." She couldn't count the nights she'd sobbed herself to sleep wanting to feel her mother's touch.

Mahalia's deep-throated cry circled the church.

"Sometimes I feel like a motherless chile," sang the choir's senior member, nodding her head toward Mahalia, passing the torch back to her.

"Sometimes I feel like I'm almost gone." Mahalia's big voice pushed against the church's roof.

"Far, far away from home, a long, long ways from home," sang the choir, congregation, minister, men, women, and children. They laid hold of Mahalia's voice. She pulled them along with:

Sometimes I feel like a motherless chile,
Sometimes I feel like a motherless chile,

Far, far away from home, a—long ways from home,
Then I get down on my knees an' pray—
Get down on my knees an' pray.

Mount Moriah rocked with Mahalia. The song overflowed into Water Street. Passersby stopped and sang. Inside the church, people swung with the music and the words, to and fro, from side to side, in rhythm. Whitehaired women, too old to sway, snapped their fingers. The sound was like seeds in dried pods, crackling beneath the spirited singing. Mahalia cut loose. People clapped their hands as though they held tambourines. Some moaned, some groaned, the moans and groans alternating with the hand-clapping and feet-patting in West African rhythms. Mahalia sank to her knees. The congregation wept. For a moment Mahalia had freed her people. At sixteen she was the kind of singer the Baptists called a "church wrecker." She had sung "Motherless Child" and torn up Mount Moriah. And when the "Thank you, Jesus . . . Thank you, Jesus . . ." came from the lips of the faithful, they were showing their appreciation for Mahalia's song, cleansing frustration from their hearts.

She remained on her knees. Her faith in God was as stout as David's when he called for heavenly help to get Goliath off Israel's back. But God gave Mahalia no clear answer on whether she should go to Chicago.

When the service ended, Mahalia and Hannah waited outside for Aunt Duke, who had stayed a moment to settle some club affairs.

"Beautiful song, Sister Haley," said one of the departing congregation.

"God's own gift," said another.

Mahalia's face lit up. The words of praise made her forget that her feet hurt and that her dress was too tight. For a moment she didn't know whether she really wanted to leave New Orleans. Go away from her closest friends, dearest relatives, her home, to face the unknown? Leaving Water Street for the cold windy city could be dangerous, as dangerous as moving to Water Street from the Gump-stump plantation had been for her mother.

"What's keeping Duke?" Hannah complained.

"She never feels right till she sees that everyone's out," said Mahalia.

"Here she comes with Emanuel," said Hannah. They started for home.

When they neared the house, Mahalia smelled the collard greens and salt pork Aunt Duke had left on the back of the stove. They went in.

Aunt Duke hurried to the kitchen. Mahalia heard her lift the lid of the stove to put in a piece of firewood. Mahalia put on her apron. She hoped Hannah would stay out of the kitchen, so she could tell Aunt Duke she had made up her mind.

⊷ 5 ⊱

Chicago, Here I Come

The train for Chicago was in the station when Mahalia and Hannah got there. Mahalia heard the locomotive's steam exploding. Any minute now the conductor would cry, "All aboard!"

Mahalia and Hannah hurried to the end of the line at the closed Jim Crow ticket window. Mahalia's traveling had been limited to a few Sunday school excursions on the Mississippi. Her heart pounded.

If only the ticket agent would come! That's what came from having to wait till the last moment to leave Water Street, with Aunt Duke hanging on to her as though going to Chicago was certain death. Even if they got their tickets in time, they'd still have to run for their lives to get to the Jim Crow coach. It was always at the far end of the platform.

The line at the window got longer. The ticket agent had to man both white and black windows. He was still taking care of the white people. After he finished there, he'd take his own sweet time to open the black window.

"Baby Dodd, you hold onto Helen's hand. Mind now, you children got to look after one another," said an overburdened mother behind Mahalia. The woman had a baby in her arms and three other children, ranging from five to ten years in age, each of whom carried a bundle. Mahalia wondered how far the woman could travel without help. Hannah was becoming angry at the delay. But she hadn't forgotten that a black had to keep quiet in New Orleans.

Mahalia sighed.

"Don't take it too hard," Hannah said. "You know your Aunt Duke is as stubborn as a blue-nosed mule. She'll forgive you for leaving after you get settled in church."

"I feel rotten," said Mahalia.

"Never mind. If we can get old slowpoke to sell us our tickets, we'll be on our way," said Hannah.

They heard the ticket agent fumbling with coins behind the closed window. Finally he opened the window.

He was a young man with a thin red moustache. He addressed each purchaser by any name he felt like. "Well, Aunt Sarah, you goin' all the way up North? Here's your ticket. Now don't lose it. Your change. Can you count? Smart nigger."

"One of these days you're goin' to be late for your own funeral and keep the devil waitin' for your soul," said Hannah. She placed the money for their tickets before the agent.

"Nigger woman, if you sass me anymore, I won't even sell you a ticket." His voice grated on Mahalia. She watched him shoot a long stream of brown tobacco juice toward the spittoon, and miss.

"Where you gals goin'?" he asked, wiping the corner of his mouth with the back of his hand.

"Chicago," said Hannah.

"Nigger-lovin' Chicago and welcome to them."

Hannah held her tongue.

"Round trip? Or one way?"

"One way."

They picked up their luggage and lunchbasket and hurried to their coach. It was filthy as usual. The Chickenbone Express, blacks called it, on account of the bones littering the floor from the lunches they ate on their way North.

Finally all the passengers were aboard. Mahalia saw that the overburdened mother and her children had found places at one end of the coach beside the door.

Mahalia heard the locomotive's warning whistle. Its bell clanged. She felt the train jerk forward. At last she was on her way to Chicago. She took the advertisement about the nurses' training school out of her sweater pocket. She had clipped it from the *Chicago Defender*. She had read it so many times that she knew it by heart.

Provident Hospital and Training School for Nurses offers young colored women a three-year course in the practice and theory of nursing. Graduates eligible for registration from any state. Classes now forming. For information apply to Superintendent, Provident Hospital, 16 West 36 Street, Chicago, Illinois.

Mahalia put the scrap of paper back in her pocket, next to her train ticket. Like the ticket, it would furnish her a chance to improve her lot, she hoped. And yet she worried about being eligible. Did just finishing that dinky little school in New Orleans make her a graduate? Would they accept her in Chicago?

She saw that Hannah had been watching her out of the corner of her eye. "You've got to get some decent clothes. You can't let those Provident people see you looking like a field hand," Hannah said.

Mahalia looked at her sweater. She didn't own a winter coat. The sweater over her jacket would have to keep her warm until she got a job and saved enough money to get a coat, she thought. She had to admit the sweater and her heavy shoes did make her look like a country black at a tent meeting. But she wasn't going to let that keep her from becoming a nurse. Lord knows, she had nursed enough children and adults too for almost nothing a week to entitle her to make a living at it.

Lord, how many miles will I have to travel to get where I want to be? To get rid of this scared, cold, unwanted feeling? Will I always be like that little boll weevil, looking for a home? She wanted a home—or at least a room of her own. Privacy. Where she could listen to Bessie Smith's records and sing when she felt like it and as loud as she wanted to without someone reminding her that she was doing something bad.

Hannah interrupted her daydreaming. "I'm hungry." She took the cover off the basket of food Aunt Duke had prepared for them so at least they'd have a full belly when they got to Chicago.

"So am I," said Mahalia. Her spirits rose when she saw the crisp brown fried chicken, baked yams, and biscuits. "Give me a drumstick and one of those buttermilk biscuits, please."

"Lord have mercy, the biscuits are still warm," said Hannah.

Mahalia blessed the food. They ate in silence while the train chugged northward, parallel to the muddy Mississippi.

Darkness fell. The train picked up speed, clicking over the cold rails. Mahalia listened to the voices whispering in the car. She finished eating and helped Hannah tidy up the basket. She closed her eyes. A man twanged a guitar while he held the blade of a knife on the steel strings and began singing:

> *I'm tired of this Jim Crow, gonna leave this Jim*
> *   Crow town,*
> *Doggone my black soul, I'm sweet Chicago bound,*
> *Yes, I'm leavin' here, from this old Jim Crow town.*
> *I'm goin' up North, where they say money grows on*
> *   trees,*

I don't give a doggone, if ma black soul leaves,
I'm goin' where I don't need my B.V.D.'s.

Mahalia smiled. The man went on singing. At last she fell asleep.

A baby's crying woke her. At first she thought the baby was sick. She made her way down the aisle to see. "Can I help?" she asked the mother.

"We'll make out. My baby's cold, I guess."

Mahalia wondered what to do. Then she took her sweater off and gave it to the woman.

"Bless you," said the mother.

Mahalia went back to her seat. She tried to sleep, but the cold kept her awake. She watched the red reflections and black shadows, cast from the fire in the locomotive's boilers, race alongside her window. Suddenly the red glow lit up a line of lopsided shanties with tin roofs. Each had a chicken coop on one side, a little garden of frost-bitten collard and turnip greens on the other, and a pig rooting nearby. They were like the shanties on Water Street.

In the morning the woman returned Mahalia's sweater.

"You can't go round Chicago giving away your only sweater to a stranger," said Hannah as they ate their breakfast from the leftovers in their basket.

Mahalia chewed and listened.

"Chicago's different. With different kinds of strangers," Hannah said. "Take New Orleans. You get the notion that all those whites worry about is how to keep blacks down and out of sight.

"In Chicago, whites are so busy getting ahead they don't seem to worry about blacks. That is, till a black tries to buy a home in a white neighborhood, or tries to get a good job beside a white man." Hannah started getting their luggage from the rack above them.

The train slowed down as it came into a vast network of railroad tracks with more trains and box cars than anyone could count. Beyond the tracks were the tallest buildings Mahalia had ever seen.

⊰6⊱

South Side

"A friend said he'd pick us up. I got to phone him. Watch our bags," said Hannah in the depot. "You got to keep your eyes open at all times, or someone will steal from you. You're in Chicago."

Soon she was back. She started toward the lunch counter. "We'll get a cup of coffee," she said.

Mahalia followed her. She didn't see any black people sitting at the counter. Maybe they wouldn't be served. A black couldn't get a drink of water in a New Orleans coffee shop, even if he was dying of thirst. She hoped Hannah knew what she was doing.

"Here's two seats. Put your bag down and sit," said Hannah. Mahalia sat beside her. On the other side was a white woman who continued to stare at her cup of coffee. When Hannah signaled the white waitress, Mahalia felt more and more uncomfortable.

"Two cups of coffee," said Hannah.

"Black or white?" The waitress quickly picked up two cups and held them beside the milk spigot. Mahalia was puzzled. Black or white? The waitress could see they were black. Hannah ordered milk for their coffees, and Mahalia understood there had been no reference to the color of their skin. It was the first time she had ever been served by a white person in a public place.

"I couldn't reach my friend. We'll have to get a cab," Hannah said as they left the station.

A cab driven by a white man stopped, and Hannah got in. Mahalia got in beside her. It was against the law in New Orleans for a black person to ride in a cab driven by a white man. The cabbie put their luggage in the trunk. Hannah gave him her address. They started out with the motor backfiring and the brakes squealing. People rushed along the sidewalks as though fleeing from the devil. Why were they in such a hurry?

"Haley, I've been thinking about you wanting to be a nurse." Hannah cleared her throat.

"Yes'm," said Mahalia.

"You're only sixteen. Maybe you ought'n aim so high at the start."

Mahalia remained silent.

"Us Clark women have never done anything but wash

white folks' dirty clothes, take care of their brats, cook for them, and scrub their floors," said Hannah.

The cab turned north.

"There's a good living to be made washing and straightening black women's hair. It don't take long to learn, and then you could set up your own shop," said Hannah.

"I'll think about it," Mahalia said.

"If you don't take to that, maybe you'd like to go into embalming," said Hannah.

"Embalming dead people?" asked Mahalia.

"Some black undertakers are hiring women to embalm women," said Hannah.

"I want to help heal live people. As a nurse I might be able to do that," Mahalia told her.

They rode along in silence until they came to where Mahalia saw many more black people on the streets than before.

"Rich blacks live over there where you see doormen in front of the apartment entrances," Hannah said.

"Are they friendly?" Mahalia asked.

" 'Bout as friendly as rich whites."

"How'd they make their money?"

"Some made it from banks. Real honest-to-goodness banks. Some made it from policy banks."

"Policy banks—you mean gambling?"

"From gambling," said Hannah.

"What's that I smell?" Mahalia next asked.

"That's the stockyards. That's where they kill hogs and cattle," said Hannah.

"What's that building over there?" Mahalia pointed.

"That's part of Chicago University."

They rode through a park and came out on the street again.

"Over there is Provident Hospital," said Hannah.

"Provident?" There was a note of awe in Mahalia's voice.

"They've got a black doctor there, Dr. Dan, who operated on a man's heart and saved his life," said Hannah.

"He must be a wonderful man," said Mahalia.

"And that's the Regal Theatre where Bessie Smith sings when she's in Chicago," said Hannah.

"I've got to hear Bessie," said Mahalia. "How much does a ticket cost?"

"One dollar."

Here was black Chicago—the South Side ghetto, second only to Harlem—in the boom days of the late 1920's. Some of the apartment houses with smartly uniformed doormen that black people lived in were finer than the properties of wealthy whites in New Orleans. Mahalia was all eyes as her aunt named the imposing churches owned by black congregations. There was Greater Salem Baptist Church, which Hannah and Alice attended. Hannah hoped Mahalia would go there. Mahalia shook her head. She wasn't sure. She wanted to attend a church where the singing was right. And by "right" she meant the way they sang at Mount Moriah. She didn't want anything fancy to get between the way she sang, and she had heard about the way blacks sang when they came North, as if they were ashamed of anyone knowing they came from the South.

Hannah pointed out black-owned businesses. Some of them were prosperous, like the *Chicago Defender*—the world's leading black weekly. Mahalia saw offices of black doctors, dentists, lawyers, undertakers. A black policeman directed traffic right there at a busy intersection. A black cop! Mahalia had never seen one before. Hannah talked about black women who worked as hotel maids, earning twelve dollars a week with two hot meals on the job—and tips! The South Side even had its own black congressman, Oscar DePriest—born in Alabama. He had just been elected. For the first time in the nation's history a northern black sat in Congress. The last southern black elected to Congress from the South had left in 1901. If an Alabama-born black could be sent to Washington as a congressman from Chicago, Hannah had heard people say, then not only could a black cow eat green grass and give white milk—but anything was possible.

Finally they came to Hannah's apartment house. When they went in, Mahalia took a deep breath. She didn't like the smell of the place. Someone was cooking something that didn't smell as though it should be eaten. She waited in the dim hall while Hannah found the key to her apartment. She felt anxious and afraid.

Hannah showed Mahalia the room Aunt Alice had. Then the tiny living room and the couch Hannah slept on.

They went on past a room rented to a railroad dining-car waiter. Then they came to the dining room. Here Alice's little son, Nathaniel, had a bed. Finally Hannah showed Mahalia a sun porch. There was a couch in the drafty room. Here Mahalia was to sleep.

Hannah left to start dinner. Mahalia sat down on the couch. She heard her Aunt Alice come into the apartment and rushed out to greet her. Something was wrong. Alice said she had lost her job. When they sat down to the hot dogs and mush, gloom sat with them. A friend of Alice's had given her the names of people who needed laundresses. That was what Alice planned to do. She gave Mahalia one of the names. If they got enough laundry work and Hannah kept her job, they'd make out.

"The apartment rent is fifty a month," said Hannah.

"Fifty dollars?" Mahalia wasn't sure she had understood what Hannah said.

"Fifty dollars. Our lodger's rent pays for the gas and electricity," said Hannah.

"I'll pay my share," said Mahalia.

❧ 7 ❧

Washing White Folks' Clothes

It was still dark and bitter cold the next morning when Mahalia and Alice left for work. Mahalia was to reach her job by the elevated train. "Count fifteen stops. Then get off and take a crosstown train for five more stops," Alice told her.

When the train came and Mahalia got on, she looked up and down the length of the car, hoping to find a black passenger. She wanted to sit beside another black. If she needed help in finding her way, she'd have someone to ask. But she had to settle for a seat between two white workmen. She expected them to protest, but they didn't look up from their newspapers.

The train rumbled along. Suddenly Mahalia was terrified—she had forgotten to count the stops! She was supposed to stay on for fifteen of them! How many had she already passed? The first streaks of morning light grayed the train's dirty windows. The train came to another stop. She watched the people inside trying to get out as those on the outside pushed forward. She decided she had passed five stops and began counting the next ones: six, seven, eight. What if she were wrong? Well, at least she remembered the woman's name and address.

When the train came to what she thought was her stop, she got out and waited for the crosstown one. When it came, she looked around for a seat, and again began counting the stops. After five stops she got off and went down to the street. She looked for Herndon Avenue and found it. She was hungry. She hoped the people would give her a cup of coffee. She hadn't had breakfast.

She rang the doorbell. While she waited, the smell of fresh coffee made her mouth water. A woman's plump, tired face appeared at the door. Mahalia told her she had come to do the laundry. The woman pointed to a door leading to the basement. Mahalia let herself into the cold laundry. She saw a mountain of soiled clothing in one corner. Sheets, pillowcases, tablecloths, children's clothing, and whatnot.

The door at the top of a flight of stairs opened, and the plump tired-faced woman came halfway down, leaving the door open. Breakfast smells followed her. She looked at Mahalia.

"Yes, you'll do. My name is Mrs. Smith. What's yours?"

"Mahalia Jackson."

"Mahalia, I'll pay you a dollar a day and carfare. The tubs, washboard, soap, and boilers are over there behind the furnace," Mrs. Smith said.

Mahalia saw her tools. She took off her sweater and rolled up her sleeves.

"I'd like you to come tomorrow to iron. It's my day to play bridge with the girls," said Mrs. Smith.

"Yes'm," said Mahalia.

"While you're ironing, you can also keep an eye on the children," Mrs. Smith said. Turning, she went back upstairs closing the kitchen door behind her.

Mahalia filled the tubs and set to work. The coarse soap bit into the raw flesh. She tried to remember her favorite song—her laundry song. But she was so cold and hungry, it was hard to concentrate on the words of "His Eye Is on the Sparrow." Her teeth chattered.

She began, "His eye is on the sparrow / And I know He watches me. / I sing because I'm free." But that wasn't the way the song began. She rubbed a while longer till the beginning came to her: "Why should I be discouraged? / Why should the shadows come? / Why should my heart be lonely, / And long for heav'n and home? / When love is my portion, / A constant friend to me."

"Sing me another song."

Mahalia looked up at the stairs leading to the kitchen. A small girl was sitting there. She smiled. Mahalia began another song.

"What on earth are you doing on the steps?" asked

Mrs. Smith. She stood in the doorway, looking down at her daughter.

"Listening to her sing," the child said.

"You do have a beautiful voice," said Mrs. Smith.

"Thank you," said Mahalia.

When lunchtime came, Mrs. Smith appeared with a plate of food. After Mahalia finished eating, she returned to work. Her first day went pretty much the way work went in New Orleans—from sunup to sundown. She earned twenty-five cents more than she had in New Orleans.

As she walked from the elevated train to Hannah's apartment house that night, Mahalia looked for a church to join, one where she would feel at ease and could sing the way she liked. If she saw that a gospel choir was on the program posted outside, that would be her church. At that time most churches had two choirs. The gospel choir was made up of men and women whose voices weren't trained. They sang the old-time spirituals the way their parents had sung them, and when they got happy, they weren't ashamed to clap, pat their feet, or shout.

Mahalia read the list of the most popular blues songs of the day posted on the window of a record shop: "Boll Weevil Blues," "Back Water Blues," "Blue Devil Blues," "Black Snake Blues," "Basin Street Blues," "Jobless Blues," "Eviction Blues," "Landlord Blues," "Howling Cat Blues," "St. Louis Blues. . . ."

She wanted a place of her own where she could have a phonograph. Then she could listen to some blues without feeling guilty. Wasn't no sin to listen to blues. She certainly didn't want to sing them. Surely God wouldn't mind if she listened to the blues once in a while. He understood how even church people could sometimes feel blue, blue as she felt then.

Chicago was enough to give anyone the blues. People didn't seem to have time to stop and ask how you felt. They didn't have time to smile. She missed New Orleans' daily ritual of courtesy.

Mahalia stopped outside a lighted church. She listened to the people singing. No, this one wouldn't do. The singing seemed cold. Maybe the city did something to the voices of black people.

She hurried home. She'd look again the next evening on her way home from work. She entered the apartment with the key Hannah had given her. Her aunt Alice met her in the hall. She was crying.

"Hannah has had a heart attack," she said. Alice had called the doctor. He came and gave Hannah some pills. Hannah was asleep now. They didn't know whether she would live.

Alice and Mahalia looked in at Hannah; then Mahalia went to her room. She knelt beside her couch, and prayed for Hannah's recovery.

⋖ 8 ⋗

The Bottom Falls Out

Mahalia found the right church. It was the one that Hannah, now well again, and Alice went to—the Greater Salem Baptist Church. It reminded her of the psalm: "In Judah is God known: His name is great in Israel. In Salem also is his tabernacle, and his dwelling place in Zion."

All she had to offer was a big voice, and she was happy when she was invited to try out for the choir. There were fifty men and women in it. They sang from songbooks. Some of them seemed to have had voice training. Mahalia watched while the choirmaster put them through their paces.

Mahalia could not read music. She knew nothing

about harmony or the structure of chords. She had learned to sing by listening to birds sing and to music—to the spirituals she had heard in church, to street vendors, to the records of Ma Rainey and Bessie Smith. Blues singers had helped her learn to sing. Was that bad? As she waited for her tryout that night, Mahalia wondered if God would punish her for learning to sing His songs, songs in praise of goodness and right living, by having listened to the songs of the unsaved and the wicked.

She had never sung with a pianist. They did not have a piano in the churches where she had sung. Listening to records had taught her that every instrumentalist has a special way of tackling a song, just as every singer has her own way of singing it. Down deep inside her, if she put her mind to it, she could get the music to come out right. Her sense of hearing was a marvelously accurate recording instrument, with this difference—whatever she sang that she had learned by ear came out colored by her deep reverence for God. It was enriched by her trials and tribulations, by her gratefulness for being alive in this church this night. Never mind the pronunciation of the words. She sensed she was about to embark on a career that would lead up and up. . . . She whispered to herself, "Dear God, it's got to come tonight." She waited for the choirmaster to call her.

"Miss Mahalia Jackson," he said.

Panic took hold of her. She couldn't move. She was a long way from getting to be a trained nurse. But she wanted to help heal her people. Wanted Hannah to get well. If only God would give her the healing voice to-night!

"Miss Jackson."

She sat up. "Here goes nothing," she whispered. She took her place beside the piano. The choirmaster gave her some music. "Han' Me Down Yo' Silvah Trumpet, Gabriel" was the title of the song. She looked at the man who was going to accompany her. He was a black man. She was a black girl trying to win a place in a black choir in a black church. If she failed, her people would not make her feel ashamed.

The piano sounded far away. Mahalia whispered the first words, so that she could get the range allowed her voice by the acoustics of the room:

> *Oh, han' me down, han' me down,*
> *Han' me down yo' sil-vah trump-et, Ga-briel.*
> *Han' me down, han' me down,*
> *Han' me down yo' sil-vah trumpet, Lord, O Lord.*
> *Oh, you see dat sis-tah, dress'd so fine,*
> *Han' me down you sil-vah trump-et, Ga-briel.*
> *She ain't got Je-sus on her min'.*
> *Han' me down yo' sil-vah trump-et, Lord. . . .*

By the time she had finished the first verse, the choir room was filled with people who had come from all parts of the church when they heard her voice. The sound had even brought people in from the street. Mahalia let go with another round of "Han' Me Down Yo' Silvah Trumpet, Gabriel," her voice again a summons to the faithful.

Three weeks after Mahalia's arrival in Chicago, she

had won a place in Greater Salem's choir. Just as eleven years earlier, Mount Moriah in New Orleans had taken her in. But this time she was made a soloist. She used to say later that it was because she sang louder than anyone else.

The black Baptist church has been blessed by a long line of musical talent. It has offered budding artists opportunity to develop before an appreciative and sympathetic audience. It wasn't long before Mahalia was also singing in a quintet with four other young people. Its members included the minister's three sons—Prince, Robert, and Wilbur Johnson—and another girl, Louise Barry. They called themselves the Johnson Gospel Singers.

The quintet was fun. The teen-agers sang and put on skits to lighten the church's more somber program of saving souls. Soon they were singing all over the South Side and even at churches in downstate Illinois and Indiana. They never dreamed of earning a lot of money. And they didn't. Like Mahalia, they all scrambled for work to keep eating. For this was a time of great trouble. In the same month that Mahalia turned seventeen—October 1929—the bottom fell out of the stock market. It triggered the Great Depression throughout America and around the world. Within two months several million people were out of work. Banks closed by the hundreds. City treasuries went broke. Chicago stopped paying its schoolteachers. Children, hungry and shoeless, stayed home. Reporters wrote that the suffering among Chicago's unemployed was worse than in any other city. Young and old roamed the countryside, searching for work and food. Shanty towns called Hoovervilles sprang up everywhere. Here the homeless lived in primitive shelters made of tar paper and tin. Breadlines and soup kitchens were set up where hungry Americans got free food.

In less than two years, half the country's blacks were without jobs, a much higher rate than among whites. And where public relief was granted, blacks got less than whites. The lives that blacks had tried to build for themselves in the city of hope fell apart. Before Chicago factories laid off their white workers, they fired the blacks, who had been the last to be hired. These were the same blacks who had fled the hand-to-mouth life of sharecropping in southern cotton fields. In Chicago for the first time they had felt hard cash in their pockets on payday. They had made more money than they ever had before—while they worked. But they knew in their bones that something had to be wrong, that good times could not last. And then, the whole thing blew up in their faces. They left the factories knowing they should not have dared to dream. Some would never dream again.

Mahalia saw the shocked blacks moving slowly through Chicago's ghetto, looking for a job, any kind of work. She gave up her own plans to go to nursing school. Black churches were hard hit. Without jobs members could no longer support their pastor and the church. Yet with every agency in the ghetto going down the drain, the minister's leadership was even more urgently needed.

At first government and business leaders thought that

if they did nothing, the depression would go away like a nightmare. It was then that religious leaders like the Reverend Johnson at Greater Salem Baptist marshaled their more fortunate members to feed, clothe, house, and nurse the jobless. Anyone in need of help came to the church.

Which way could Mahalia and her kin turn? They could not afford to return to New Orleans. They could not afford to stay in Chicago. It was as Aunt Duke predicted: Out of the frying pan into the fire. The city of hope had become a trap. She thought of the Bible's words: ". . . but from him that hath not shall be taken away even that which he hath."

◦§9§◦

Music Lesson

Mahalia's day was divided by the number of buckets she had to carry to fill tubs. She soaped soiled clothing on a corrugated washboard and rubbed the dirt out of them, rinsing the clothes in water with blueing in it. Some of the more soiled things had to be placed in boiling water. Then there was the wringing of the clothes through hand-operated wringers. And then hanging the clothes on a line to dry in the harsh wind blowing off Lake Michigan.

Tomorrow, God willing, she'd return and iron the rough-dry laundry. Now she was getting a dollar and fifty cents a day—twice what she had earned in New Orleans. It was good money she thought as she boarded her train, even though it cost twice as much to live in Chicago.

With her share of the free-will offering she got for singing with the Johnson Gospel Singers, she was doing better than some black men who still hung onto jobs and had families to support. But would she be stuck at a washtub the rest of her life? After giving Alice and Hannah her share of the food and rent money, she still had a dollar or two for herself.

People—she was sure they all meant well—were forever saying: "Mahalia, you ought not let your voice go to waste. You ought to take singing lessons. There's that Professor DuBois round the corner who used to be a concert singer. Maybe he'll train you?" Well, she was going to take their advice. But her mind was against it. Something told her she'd get hurt. If she hadn't promised Louise Barry, who was going with her to find out if she, too, could take lessons, she wouldn't go through with it. A promise is a promise. She and Louise were going to take their first lesson this very same night. She had her four dollars for the lesson. Four dollars was a lot of money.

The train roared into the South Side station. It stopped, and Mahalia got off with the suds busters and range breakers—black women who like herself counted themselves lucky to have domestic work during the Great Depression's dark days. When she reached the street she found it jammed with people. The crowd was silently staring at the hunger marchers. Her heart beat faster as she watched row after row of black men, women carrying babies, children, moving slowly down the middle of the street. Their shabby clothing looked even shabbier in the gray evening light. Police mounted on skittery horses rode alongside the marchers, who carried handmade signs reading:

JOIN THE HUNGER MARCH.
PROTEST FIRINGS OF BLACKS.
GIVE US FOOD.
PROTEST EVICTIONS OF OUR FAMILIES.
DON'T BUY WHERE YOU CAN'T WORK.

A few days ago police had shot into the ranks of some hunger marchers. Five people had been killed.

Mahalia fought her way through the packed pavement toward Greater Salem. She made some progress till she came to where the sheriff's deputies were taking the furniture out of a house and putting it in the street. An eviction. As quickly as the deputies carried the battered furniture into the street, members of Marcus Garvey's United Negro Improvement Association carried it back into the house. Garvey's men outnumbered the white officials, as did the crowd watching. The Garveyites won the contest. The tenants could stay another night. Tomorrow?

Mahalia continued on her way, wondering if she shouldn't give her four dollars to the family for their rent. But the money spent on the music lesson might help her make a larger contribution later on. She helped raise money for the poor when she sang solo for Greater Salem. And so did her singing with the Johnson Gospel Singers in the little storefront churches. Anyhow she had already made the appointment with Professor DuBois. He'd charge her whether she came or not.

When she got within sight of Greater Salem Baptist Church, Mahalia saw a line of people standing at the basement entrance to the church cafeteria. They were waiting until those inside had finished eating and there was room at the tables. She went to another entrance, and once inside, found Robert, Wilbur, Prince, and Louise.

Mahalia took off her coat and joined her friends behind the steam table. Mahalia's mouth watered at the sight of the food. She felt hungrier than the marchers. But she couldn't eat till she helped with the serving. That was their job. Some of the church members went from market to market getting donations of food from sympathetic merchants. Some delivered the food to the church in their trucks. Some cooked the food. Some washed the pots and pans. No one got paid. It was the way they helped themselves. Greater Salem had become a busy relief agency that brought blacks closer together.

Tonight the very sight of the cooked food on the steam table made her so hungry she could hardly talk. She swallowed as she looked at the pigs' tails in sauerkraut, sweet potatoes, red and white beans, rice and black-eyed beans, bread pudding. The smell of freshly brewed coffee was almost her undoing.

"Mahalia, you look so sad," said Louise.

"Yes, why such a gloomy face? You're the one who picks us up when we're down," said Prince.

"I just saw the hunger marchers," said Mahalia.

"Starvation in a land of plenty. It's a crime," said Robert.

"In the South all we had to do was keep out of the way of whites and fight hard times. We usually had a little garden of collards, some chickens, and maybe a pig to help us stay alive," said Mahalia.

"What it all boils down to is that this depression proves once again that blacks better learn how to take care of their own," said Prince.

"If we could only get that message into our songs while we make our rounds," said Louise.

"With a few verses thrown in on how we ought to begin our own businesses to give our own people jobs so we won't have to depend on whites," said Wilbur.

"Say, what time do you two prima donnas have to take your music lesson?" asked Prince.

"Eight. And we'd better get our dinner so we won't be late." Louise looked at the clock.

Mahalia and Louise put food on their trays and went to a nearby table to eat.

"I might as well go into the lion's den with a hearty meal under my belt," Mahalia said.

"Don't worry, you'll become Professor DuBois's star pupil," Louise said.

"I'm scared."

"Mahalia, you're the Johnson Gospel Singers' star," said Louise.

After their meal the girls left for Professor DuBois's studio. The professor was finishing a lesson with another young woman. When she left, he turned to Louise and Mahalia.

"You're Miss Jackson?" asked the professor.

"Yes, sir." Mahalia had misgivings. The music teacher, a tall, light-skinned man, had such a grand manner. He spoke in a stilted voice. She didn't like him and was certain he didn't like her.

"And you're Miss Barry." He sat down at the piano. "What would you like to sing, Miss Jackson, so I can hear what sort of voice you have?"

"I'd like to sing one of those songs we used to sing down home when I was a kid," said Mahalia. She took her place near the piano, eyeing it as though it were some kind of monster out to keep her from feeling free to sing. Oh, how she longed for a pipe organ! At Greater Salem the organ in the background let her do all the little improvisations she loved to try with a song.

"What part of the South are you from?"

"New Orleans."

"That's the trouble with blacks. You can get them out of the South. But you can't get the South out of them when they come North. Here's something." He handed her a spiritual, "Standing in the Need of Prayer." Mahalia stared blindly at the black notes on the sheet. She did not know how to read music, but she knew the song. She had sung it many times at Mount Moriah Baptist

Church. As she watched the professor's hands hover over the keys, she reached back into her memory for the words and music.

The teacher began playing. She took a deep breath and began: "It's me, it's me, O Lawd. . . ."

The professor shook his head.

". . . Standin' in de need of pray'r—" Mahalia was cut off by the professor dropping both hands on the keyboard with a bang.

"That's not the way!" he said, and he showed her how, clasping his hands in front of him and singing it slowly, sadly.

"Now you try it, Miss Barry." Professor DuBois took the sheet of music from Mahalia and handed it to her friend. He began playing. Mahalia watched her friend take a deep breath and begin:

> *It's me, it's me, it's me, O Lord, Standing in the need*
> *of pray'r;*
> *It's me, it's me, it's me, O Lord, Standing in the need*
> *of pray'r.*
> *Not my brother, but it's me, O Lord, Standing in the*
> *need of pray'r;*
> *Not my sister, but it's me, O Lord, Standing in the*
> *need of pray'r.*

Louise went through it, singing each word distinctly, imitating the professor. She had a sweet voice.

"Do you hear what I mean, Miss Jackson? That young lady has a fine voice. She can be trained to be a great singer. Now let's give you another chance at it." He began playing and Mahalia sang again, the rhythm inside her making her pick up the beat.

Professor DuBois angrily banged the piano. "Please stop hollering! I want you to try pronouncing the words so white people can understand you. You sing in a way that makes the Negro race ashamed of you. . . ."

"I—" Mahalia began.

"You do everything wrong. Besides mispronouncing the words, you breathe at the wrong time; you hold the wrong notes too long."

Mahalia got her coat. She took the four dollars out of her pocketbook and handed it over.

On the way home Louise said she wanted to take more lessons as soon as she could.

Mahalia shook her head. This wasn't for her. She was black. Why should she sing songs the way white folks liked? She couldn't stand the professor's formal style. That kind of singing didn't make her feel good.

It was the first—and last—lesson she ever took.

~§ *10* §~

Making a Vow

Twenty-five dollars!

Mahalia came out of the Decca recording company's South Side studio with the crisp one-dollar bills tightly clasped in her hand. It was almost three years after the music teacher had rejected her singing. For a moment she stood in the hot sunlight, staring at the dollar bills looking so green against the brown of her work-roughened hand. The money was a godsend. Now she could pay her share of Grandpa Paul Clark's trip from New Orleans to Chicago. She started walking to the nearby bank.

The money had been paid her for her first record. Twenty-five dollars for singing a song! Twenty-five dollars during the summer of 1934, the fifth year of the Great Depression, was a fortune. Twenty-five dollars for singing one song—"God's Gonna Separate the Wheat from the Tares." A song that she had often sung. Words that made her cry when preachers read them from the Holy Bible's Matthew, Chapter 13, Verses 25 to 30. They're about the farmer having to harvest weeds (tares) before bringing in his wheat.

She hummed the song's words:

If you never hear me sing no more,
Aw, meet me on the other shore,
God's gonna separate the wheat from the tares,
Didn't he say.

When she sang with the Johnson Gospel Singers they felt themselves lucky to divide five dollars for the evening. Decca had given her twenty-five dollars. It was a "flat fee," they said, explaining that giving her a chance to sing was something special they did to encourage blacks. She would get no royalties—no percentage of the profits—from the sale of the record.

But it was business, of course, the profitable business of making "race records" by black artists for black listeners. Once such a record as Mahalia's came alive, Decca salesmen went from door to door in the ghetto selling it. People who had neither running water nor electricity in their homes somehow scraped up enough money to buy a phonograph, which was hand-cranked in those days. Black brothers and sisters were willing to spend their last dollar for a record made by a black singer or musician.

Mahalia entered the bank and took her place at the

end of the line. She got out her bank book, something she had never had before coming to Chicago. If she'd had her own account in New Orleans, she'd not have had all the fuss over the money Aunt Duke had been saving for her. Getting it from her had been like drawing hen's teeth. Taught her a lesson.

Mahalia looked at the first entry in her book. That dollar came from baby-sitting. Another dollar below it came from singing with the Johnson group. Here was a three-dollar entry! Yes, she got that for singing at a funeral at Bob Miller's undertaking parlor. Funerals weren't as fancy in Chicago as they were in New Orleans, and instead of having a marching band for the trip to the cemetery, the family sometimes had a soloist sing the deceased's favorite hymn. That's where she came in. She had something to fall back on if the Johnson Gospel Singers broke up, which was what it seemed they were about to do.

After she had made her bank deposit, she hurried home to the dinner she knew was waiting for her. Hannah would outdo herself, putting the big pot in the little pot as Aunt Duke used to down in New Orleans.

Hannah had bought a ten-pound pail of chitterlings —hog guts was what they were. They were the cheapest meat they could eat. Nothing fancy about hog guts, but when Hannah got through with them—they were something else. Hannah scraped them under running water to clean them. Then she parboiled them in a cup of vinegar and water for an hour. She threw that water away

and started the Chicago ruffles (another name for them)
cooking in a mess of garlic, onions, hot peppers, and pars-
ley. She'd let them simmer for an hour or so, while she
made the potato salad, hot water cornbread, and salad
greens. Mahalia wondered if there'd be enough for
Grandpa Paul Clark, little Nathaniel, Alice, Hannah, and
herself, and of course, any neighbor who smelled all that
good food and happened by while they were saying the
blessing. Well, it was enough to stop the old man from
talking about slavery days.

Mahalia loved to hear the old man tell about slavery.
Grandpa Clark had been born in slavery, way back in
1856. For a man of seventy-eight, his memory was good.
When Mahalia let herself into the apartment, she quietly
closed the door behind her and stood for a moment to
get a good look at the old man sitting at the head of the
table as royally as an African king. Grandpa was telling
them about how slave masters married blacks back in
those dark days of bondage:

"When a couple found out they were in love they
went up to the big house to get the master to marry them.
And the master and his wife took them to the kitchen.
The master put a broomstick on the floor and told the
couple to stand on one side of it. The master didn't have
a Bible or nothing in his hand when he mated the couple.
We kids knew what was up. We'd heard the old folks
talking about it in Slave Row where all the blacks lived.
Well, we'd be peeping in through the kitchen door to see
the couple jump over the broomstick. And that was what

the master told the couple to do: 'Jump over the broomstick—now you man and wife.' That's the truth. That's
the truth."

"And that's why they call getting married, jumping
over the broomstick?" asked little Nathaniel.

Mahalia came in the dining room to join in the laugh-
ter.

It came to Mahalia while they were eating that after
dinner they all ought to go round the corner to the
neighborhood photographer and have a picture made with
Grandpa in the center. No, it'd be best to have a picture
made of Grandpa alone and then the group. Whichever
way, the big job was to get the old man up from the
table before he yawned and took a nap. Time he woke
up from that nap, the photographer would have closed
shop and gone home for his dinner.

After they finished the blackberry cobbler, Mahalia
saw her chance. "Grandpa, I think it would be wonderful if you come round to the photographer's with me and
have your picture taken. It'll leave us something to have
round when you're back in New Orleans," said Mahalia.

"It's awfully hot for Grandpa to go out so soon after
eating," said Hannah.

"It'll only take a minute," said Mahalia.

"Where's all this money coming from for the pictures?
Must cost all of five dollars," asked Alice.

"I got a few extra dollars," said Mahalia. Somehow
she couldn't bring herself to tell them about the record.

"I hope you didn't make one of those old trashy blues

records people are always asking you to sing?" Hannah said.

Mahalia didn't say anything.

"Tell you what, I'll go if you sing my favorite," said Grandpa Clark.

Mahalia knew his favorite. She got up from the table and began:

Steal away, steal away,
Steal away to Jesus,
Steal away, steal away home,
I ain't got long to stay here.

She stopped singing when she saw her grandfather's eyes close. "Come on, Grandpa, you can nap when we get back," Mahalia said. Finally she got them all out of the apartment and to the photographer's.

After a bit of argument the photographer got the old man seated in front of his camera.

"Give us a great big smile," the photographer said.

"I don't 'xactly feel like smiling," Grandpa said.

Mahalia tried to get him to smile but he shook his head and slowly slid out of the chair. He lay on the floor with his eyes closed.

"Grandpa! Grandpa!" Mahalia rushed to pick him up from the floor.

"Don't touch him. Call an ambulance!" shouted the photographer, reaching for his telephone.

In a short time an ambulance screeched to a stop in front of the studio. Orderlies rushed in and put Grandpa Clark's limp body on a stretcher and carried the stretcher to the ambulance. Slowly the bell clanged while the ambulance rushed off to the hospital. It was too much for Mahalia. It was as though Grandpa was already dead and the ambulance was a hearse. She hailed a cab. She had to get two cabs to get the family to the hospital. When they got there, doctors had already examined Grandpa Clark. He was still unconscious. They said he might not live through the night.

Mahalia looked at her Aunt Hannah for comfort. But Hannah was crying bitterly, scared she'd lose her father.

"If you hadn't brought Grandpa out in this terrible heat this never would have happened. His death is going to be on your shoulders!" Hannah said.

It was as though Hannah had slapped her. Mahalia was too shocked to say anything. She went into the hall and walked till she found an empty room. She entered and closing the door behind her, got down on her knees. The tears flowed down her cheeks. It *was* her fault. She remembered how he had closed his eyes when she sang the line: "I ain't got long to stay here." It should have been a warning to her.

If God would only let him live! She couldn't go around the rest of her life guilty of killing him. What could she do to keep Grandpa alive? "God, if you will only let Grandpa live, I'll devote the rest of my life to the Church and doing Your bidding," Mahalia prayed. She thought of what she should give up for this miracle—it would indeed be a miracle if the old man lived. She didn't drink liquor in any form. She didn't smoke or dance.

She loved the movies and almost worshiped Charlie Chaplin, Norma Shearer, Clara Bow, Bing Crosby, Cab Calloway, the Mills Brothers. She would give up going to the movies and the theater. She made that vow and prayed a few minutes more before returning to her grandfather's room.

Mahalia repeated her vow the next day, and the next. For nine days she repeated her vow and prayed for her grandfather's recovery.

On the ninth day the old man came out of the coma. It wasn't long before he walked out of the hospital well and strong. He returned to New Orleans where he lived out his days.

❧ 11 ❧

Jumping over the Broomstick

"Don't worry about your size and weight. A lot of young men like a lot of woman. And another thing, there's a young man looking to fall in love for each woman searching for love and marriage. The problem is for them to find each other at the right time." Aunt Duke's words came back to Mahalia that night in Greater Salem Baptist Church.

She heard her name called and got up and began walking slowly to the front of the church. But it wasn't only her size that doomed her to loneliness. She thought she didn't have much of a chance of even getting a date, because she had vowed she wouldn't go to movies or to the theater. She didn't drink or dance. That just about did it. She'd have to settle for being an old maid. She was twenty-four and spending most of her spare time singing either in Greater Salem or some storefront church. Her aunts called her a church mouse.

Mahalia reached the front of the church. She nodded to the waiting pianist who played a short introduction. She cleared her throat and looked out at the congregation before closing her eyes. Then she saw a man staring at her.

Men often stared at Mahalia while she stood up in front of the congregation. She had guessed before this night that they stared at her wondering why she wasn't down on the farm plowing forty acres with a mule or out bear hunting with nothing but her fists. But the way this distinguished-looking gentleman stared at her was different. What on earth did he see in her? Her heart fluttered. She didn't believe in love at first sight. She had to keep her mind on what she was going to sing. She wasn't going to pay him any rabbit-eared mind.

"God's gonna separate the wheat from the tares," began Mahalia. She closed her eyes as she often did when she sang before a strange audience she wasn't sure would like her. She kept her eyes closed while she searched around inside for the right sound that let her know she was singing her best. The right sound made her feel happy. She couldn't sing a song unless it did something for her. When she kept her eyes closed, she found the right music, and in the darkness she concentrated and put all her feeling into her voice.

Isaac Hockenhull, the man staring at Mahalia, was

thirty-four and known to his gambler friends as Seeing-
Eye Ike. He worked irregularly during these depression
days as a substitute postal clerk. He was on call twenty-
four hours a day if extra workers were needed to handle
the incoming mail. Substitutes earned about twenty dollars
a week. In time, if they were lucky, they might become
regulars.

Before the depression, a job in the postal service was
one of the best jobs available to blacks. Many black postal
workers were able to buy homes, send their daughters and
sons to college.

Though the federal postal service provided good jobs
for blacks and high status in the community, during the
depression it became the graveyard for a number of black
college graduates like Hockenhull. Dentists, lawyers,
teachers, even doctors, found they were stuck in the postal
service for the rest of their lives. The pay there was more
than they could earn in their chosen profession.

Before coming to Chicago, Hockenhull had attended
Tuskegee Institute in Alabama. There he studied chem-
istry and mathematics. After finishing, he went to Fisk,
planning to go into his family's cosmetics-manufacturing
company. But the family firm went bankrupt, the way a
large number of businesses did during those bad times.
And Hockenhull moved to Chicago.

When Mahalia finished her song and opened her eyes,
Hockenhull was still looking at her. She saw that he
applauded longer than the others. She had to give an

encore. He was among the admirers who clustered around afterward to congratulate her.

"I remember seeing you one time in a little storefront church," he said. "I was passing when it seemed your voice reached out and pulled me in. There you were, a big green-as-grass girl from down home, singing in that run-down place cold as a refrigerator.

"You were up there in front, telling them to clap their hands or they'd freeze to death—and finally you got some heat in there though there still wasn't any fire in the stove."

Mahalia didn't know what to say. She could have heard him talk on and on. Then he had to go and spoil it.

"But why do you waste such a wonderful voice?" he asked. Waste it? What did he mean? She worked hard so that she could sing when and where she wanted to. She'd even lost her laundry job because singing out of town made her miss a day's work. Then she'd packed dates for seven dollars a week. But she'd hated the factory. Now she was working in a hotel, cleaning thirty-three rooms a day for twelve dollars a week. She turned and walked to the refreshment table for ice cream and cake. For the rest of that evening she tried to avoid him.

"Surely it's your business where and what you sing. Still and all, I can't get over how humiliating it must have been for you that night," Hockenhull said when he got Mahalia's attention again.

"What do you mean?" she asked.

"I mean having to wait while the congregation passed the collection plate for the free-will offering. I sat there and watched those poor people dropping their pennies, nickels, dimes, and collar buttons in the plate and wondered how much of it they'd give you."

"What did you put in the collection?"

"I didn't have a plugged nickel. I was flat broke."

"I didn't mean to hurt you."

"May I walk you home?"

They went together for about a year. He kept telling her she would be a great concert artist one day. If she would let him show her the way. He asked Mahalia to marry him. She didn't know what to say, remembering that they were both poor as Job's turkey and that when poverty enters the door, love flies out the window. And even so they had more than her parents had when they met and married back in Water Street. Ike was courteous and loved her. She loved him and needed him. Yet there was ten years' difference in their ages. But wasn't it a good sign that she had met him in church? She said yes.

They were married in Hannah's apartment by the pastor of Greater Salem Baptist Church. They moved into the small apartment with Hannah, Alice, Nathaniel, and the roomer. It was a mistake. The others didn't like it when Hockenhull began locking himself in the only bathroom to experiment in the making of cosmetics and hair ointments. Once he had perfected them, he planned to have Mahalia sell these articles while on her singing engagements.

The more time he spent locked in his bathroom laboratory, the more hostile Mahalia's kin became. And the more hostile they became, the more time he spent making cosmetics. It became more and more urgent for Mahalia and her husband to move into their own apartment. Money from the cosmetics would make this possible, he said.

Hockenhull often went to the public library to spend his spare time studying the pedigrees, speed, and endurance of racehorses. He knew the size and design of every important racetrack in the country. He dreamed of owning a racehorse the way Mahalia dreamed of owning her own home.

Soon Mahalia found Hockenhull's great weakness was betting on the horses. "Why you think they call him Seeing-Eye Ike?" members of Greater Salem asked her. At first she chided herself for being so blind. How could a Christian woman from a good Baptist family not have known her man was a gambler? Well, she consoled herself, all members of the church weren't saved. It was up to her to help save him. She would pray for him. Maybe God would answer her prayers as He had when Grandpa Clark lay sick.

~§ 12 §~

Once in a Blue Moon

She'd gone to Buffalo to sing on a weekend, planning to be back at work Monday morning. On the return trip she missed her bus connection in Cleveland, and when she got back to Chicago Tuesday, the hotel fired her. Ike too had no job.

The two-room apartment they'd taken after leaving Hannah's place was too small to fight a rat in. But large enough to be cold and drafty without heat. They lived in one of the rooms; Ike used the other one to manufacture cosmetics and to analyze racing forms in search of that horse which might bring him fortune if he ever got the money to bet.

When Ike wasn't in that room, Mahalia tried her

hand at the beauty parlor business. Occasionally she washed, dried, oiled, and pressed her friends' hair. One of these days when times got better, she would go into business. Hannah had been right. Wanting to be a nurse, she had aimed too high. There was a living to be made in Chicago's ghetto in the hair-dressing business. But now she and Ike were barely able to scrape along as she did an occasional head and both of them sold his cosmetics. Wherever she sang, she took along a suitcase packed with jars of ointments and cosmetics to sell during intermission. Ike sold his concoctions from door to door. Enough money came in to buy groceries, but all too often there wasn't enough left to pay the landlord.

Mahalia had to laugh at the rumors going round in Greater Salem Church about Ike's cosmetics. Some gossip mongers claimed they weren't cosmetics but conjuring preparations made of roots and herbs for people who wanted to voodoo—do harm to—others. Some even went so far as to say that she and Ike went out to the graveyard at nights to get graveyard dirt to sell to people who wished someone bad luck. The buyer of graveyard dirt rubbed it on a glove, which was then used to shake hands with the unguarded one, bringing bad trouble.

So here on this blue evening, a day before the rent was due, Mahalia and Ike finished unpacking a box of jars to put his hair ointment in. Ike put aside the newspaper the jars were wrapped in to read later. Mahalia looked at her husband wondering how much longer were they going to live this way. She was twenty-seven; he was thirty-seven.

Would they ever get away from poverty? She had been poor so long she was used to it, but Ike's life had been different. His people had had enough money to send him to college. She wanted to have a home of her own, with flowers in the backyard, before she became too old to be able to take care of it. She was still praying for him to quit gambling. With God's help she would save him.

"Look, honey." Ike stood up with the paper in front of him.

She saw his hands tremble, so that the paper shook. "Yes, Ike. Calm yourself."

"Here's a story about a government plan to feed and take care of a group of black artists and singers stranded here in Chicago."

"What's the date of the paper?"

"I can't find the date of the paper, but just listen." He read her the story about an all-black show stranded in Chicago. There was no money for salaries. Members of the show had applied to Chicago relief authorities for food and housing. Some were sick and needed a doctor's care. The Federal Theatre, a work relief project for unemployed people in the profession, took over. It was hiring the company for an all-black production of Gilbert and Sullivan's *Mikado*.

"Imagine blacks singing Gilbert and Sullivan? What else will the white man dream up?" Ike turned the page to continue the story. The Federal Theatre people were going to call their all-black version *The Swing Mikado* because the latest thing in jazz was called swing.

"Now listen to this: 'A Chicago singer, an amateur, will be given a chance to begin her professional career in *The Swing Mikado* if she wins the audition in a contest tomorrow at the Great Northern Theatre.' "

"What date is that paper?"

Hurriedly Ike turned the pages, searching. "It's today's date, and the 'tomorrow' means you've got a chance to enter the contest."

"I don't want to enter any contest."

"Sooner or later you've got to find out if you can become a great singer."

"What do you mean?"

"You're wasting your gift."

"I sing songs that make me happy. It's my voice. If I want to sing for God on a street corner, no one will stop me." Mahalia did not know how to explain this something down deep inside her, something that whispered to her to stand firm.

"You're not only wasting your gift," Ike said, "but the way you sing spirituals makes intelligent blacks ashamed of you. And whites can't understand you."

"Singing the old spirituals for blacks who are not ashamed of being black or from the South helps me fight for my people."

"Let's look at it this way. There are not enough blacks with enough money left over from paying rent, church dues, burial-society dues, grocery bills, clothing, and so on, to support a black singer so she can make a living.

"So what do *you* have to do? You have to sing for

white people. White people have all the money. You have
to go where the money is. If you intend to make the most
of your gift, you must sing what white people want to
hear, and you must sing it the way they want to hear it
sung. Don't you understand?"

Mahalia tried to understand. She said, "I don't like
the idea of our money going to feed horses with those bets
you make—especially not with all the hungry people, in-
cluding us, around here. But I don't mess with you and
your horses. I hope the good Lord will help me help you
get rid of this gambling fever. I pray every night that
He'll show you the right path."

"Now, don't you go putting the jinx on me and my
horses. It's hard enough to pick a winner without you
setting the Lord against me. Come on, Mahalia, enter the
contest. It'll give you the training and experience you
need. Where will you get hollering those gospel songs? Besides, there isn't a dollar in the house. That theater will
pay you sixty dollars a week."

The next day Mahalia took her worn copy of the
Baptist songbook, *Gospel Pearls*, and went down to the
Great Northern Theatre. Even if she didn't know how to
read the notes, the words were in the songbook to guide
her once the pianist played a song.

She signed her name to the long list of contestants
that someone set before her. When the young woman
asked what Mahalia was going to sing, she showed her
Gospel Pearls. That wouldn't do at all, the lady said. You'd
better go buy the right kind of music.

Mahalia left the theatre. In a store window she saw "Sometimes I Feel Like a Motherless Child." That was how she felt at the moment. She bought the song and went slowly back to the theatre, hoping somebody else had already been picked. When she got there, she found that she was going on in a few moments.

They called her name. She walked out on the stage and handed the pianist the song. He put it in front of him, looked at her, and began playing. She folded her hands in front of her and closed her eyes so she wouldn't have to see the faces scattered through the vast theatre. She listened to find where she was to begin singing, but this wasn't the arrangement she was used to. The pianist stopped playing. She opened her eyes. Everyone was looking at her. The pianist shrugged and began playing again. Now that she had heard the arrangement once, she began whispering the first lines of the song. Her voice rose a notch when she thought of Charity and her death and of how she had cried herself to sleep wanting her mother's touch. And when she thought of how Aunt Duke had tried to take the place of her mother, the song sprang from her lips, searching for the theatre's roof, crying to escape into the street. She knew what it meant to feel lost and deserted.

There was no sound when Mahalia finished. She opened her eyes, hurriedly gathered her things, and left the silent theatre. She walked through the streets for a while, and then caught a streetcar. At the door Ike met her, and she began to cry.

"You won it, Mahalia! You won it!" he shouted. "They phoned to say you won! You've made it, honey!"

Mahalia sat down. She shook her head.

"And on top of that good news I've found a job," said Ike.

"A job! Then I won't have to sing in a theatre!" she said.

But Ike did not hear her. He was busy planning her career before the footlights.

"I said I'm not going to take the part," Mahalia said slowly. "Now that you've got a job, I don't have to sing in that show."

"But you won it!"

"Yes, I won it, and I also made a vow back in 1934."

"A vow in 1934? What has that to do with *The Swing Mikado*?"

"My grandfather lay at death's door, and I asked God to spare his life. I told God I would never step my foot in a theatre or sing in a place that served whisky. God spared my grandfather's life. I aim to keep my part of the bargain."

Still Ike didn't get the message. He jumped up and struck the table with his fist. He went over all the wonderful breaks that might come Mahalia's way if she took this role. In the end Mahalia would not be moved.

"Once in a blue moon an opportunity comes fitted for an artist like you. Once in a blue moon! And you let it slip through your fingers." Ike rocked his head in his hands.

Mahalia looked at Ike. She did not approve of his gambling, but she never scolded him. Why couldn't he live and let live, and not meddle with the way she had to sing?

She closed her eyes. A peace came over her. It was a pity that Ike could never understand. To her gospel singing meant broadcasting good news. It was the salvation of blacks. That was what gospel songs were. Good tidings set to music. Gospel singing connected both singer and listener in an outpouring of joyful emotion. And the joyful emotion came from both singer and listener knowing that each would overcome earthly perils and prove victorious; their reward was peace of mind. Gospel music was helping blacks survive the Great Depression. To understand this, you had to know that a gospel song was a cheering, an optimistic sermon set to music, lending splendor and beauty to listener and singer. She admired the way the older gospel singers she had met in her comings and goings, carried themselves. They sang while they lived in the ghetto's ugliness. She wanted to walk tall and upright like the older women, who walked as though marching to Zion. Ike ought to know she couldn't trade her gospel singing for all the frivolous roles in a dozen *Swing Mikados*.

Not long after, Ike's dream came true. He bet twenty on a hundred-to-one horse. The horse won, and Ike collected two thousand dollars which he brought home for Mahalia to keep till they decided where to buy a home. Mahalia hid the money under the rug before leaving for

Detroit for a singing date. When she returned, she looked for the money in its hiding place. It was gone. She was heartbroken. Why hadn't she put it in the bank? Later, when Ike came home, Mahalia was in tears. She gave him the bad news. Ike smiled and comforted her. Yes, he had found the money, and he had bought a racehorse with it.

"That's a lot of money to pay for a horse. Especially since I don't eat horsemeat," said Mahalia.

"Silly goose. This horse is not for eating. He's a racehorse."

"When will you race him? I want to know. Because I don't want that money if you win."

"In a couple of months."

"Where will you keep him? There's hardly enough room in the apartment for us. What will he eat?"

"I've put him in a boarding stable till I race him."

Mahalia did not understand—no more than Ike understood her gospel singing.

Two moods of Mahalia Jackson.   *Columbia Records Photo*

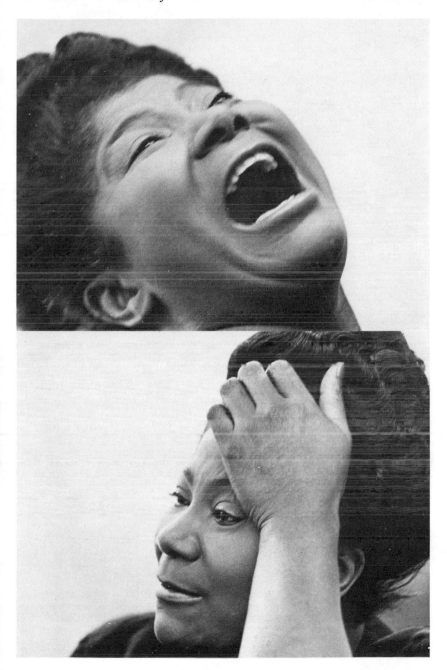

Mahalia sings at Newport, 1958.   *Maynard Frank Wolfe*

One of Mahalia's business ventures, "glori-fried" chicken.

Amsterdam News

At the dedication of a statue of the composer, W. C. Handy, Mahalia sang one of his great spirituals, "I'll Never Turn Back." Memphis, Tennessee, 1960.

Wide World Photos

Singing "The Star-Spangled Banner" at John F. Kennedy's Inaugural Ball, 1961.

Jim Brown/ Black Star

"I Been 'Buked and I Been Scorned." The March on Washington, August 28, 1963.   *Flip Schulke/Black Star*

A fund-raising concert for the Southern Christian Leadership Conference, Chicago, 1965. Mildred Falls, Mahalia's life-long friend, is the accompanist.   *Bob Fitch/Black Star*

An English reviewer wrote, "Thousands were there, but Mahalia
sang only to me." *United Press International Photo*

A concert in the Berlin Sportpalast. *United Press International Photo*

Among her many honors, the St. Vincent de Paul medal for "serving God through the needs of men," conferred by DePaul University at their commencement in 1971.

Wide World Photos

Six thousand mourners crowded into Chicago's McCormick Place for
Mahalia's funeral, February 1, 1972.   *Wide World Photos*

◄§ *13* §►

Fish-and-Bread Singer

One evening after choir practice Thomas A. Dorsey, the black composer, came to Greater Salem Baptist Church to offer Mahalia a song-plugger's job. It was the spring of 1939. The gospel-song composer was at the peak of a productive life. Before he had been brought back into the Baptist church, baptised, and saved again, he had made many sinners dance with his blues songs. When he rejoined the church, he composed religious songs as diligently as he had blues. And oddly enough these church songs also made people dance—a holy dance. Dorsey, that old blues magician, became a church magician.

As for Sister Mahalia, she was on the threshold of putting all her experiences as a gospel singer together. Her voice was at its strongest. Her gospel recordings had earned her one hundred dollars all told. The records— "God's Gonna Separate the Wheat From the Tares," "Keep Me Every Day," and "God Will Wipe All Tears Away"— had been copied without her permission, stolen by other companies. They sold well, though she did not profit by their success.

Mahalia listened to Dorsey's proposal. She wanted to know what a song-plugger did. Dorsey explained that a song-plugger is a singer employed to promote a composer's songs and induce people to buy them. Dorsey knew he could write a truckload of religious songs, but if he couldn't get them sold and sung, he might just as well not have taken the trouble. This was particularly true in 1939 when Dorsey's publishing house competed with five other firms headed by equally gifted black composers.

In 1926 Dorsey had composed his first gospel hit, "If You See My Savior, Tell Him That You Saw Me." He had five hundred copies printed, he told Mahalia. He borrowed money to mail the song to churches throughout the United States. Three years passed before he sold a single copy. When the all-black National Baptist Convention met in Chicago in 1930, Dorsey hired a girl to sing the song at the meeting in the Coliseum. When she finished singing, everyone was crying. The musical directors of the biggest Baptist organization in the land let Dorsey sell all the copies of the song he wanted to. That was what a song-plugger could do.

Dorsey, the son of a Baptist preacher, was born in a

town close to Atlanta, Georgia. Young Dorsey proved to
be a prodigy, mastering several musical instruments at an
early age—all except the piano. There was no piano in his
home or in his father's church, but a music teacher who
lived four miles away in the country had one. Dorsey
walked the four miles out for lessons and the four miles
back to his home four times a week. He learned to play
ragtime, blues, jazz, and religious music.

Dorsey fell in love with circus bands. Before the tru-
ant officer caught up with him, he had run away with a
circus to follow its music. When he left the circus, he
slipped into ghetto entertainment circles, earning $1.50 a
night stomping a piano at Saturday night dances. Before
he was twenty, he fell in love with a beautiful black girl
but was rejected by her.

He left Georgia to go North, finding a job pouring
steel in the mills of Gary, Indiana. Then he organized a
five-piece band to play at parties in the black communities
of Gary and South Chicago. He learned to make jazz arrangements for the band, and with the money he earned,
took lessons in composition at a music school in Chicago.

Dorsey joined Chicago's Pilgrim Baptist Church and
in the same year heard a gospel song, "I Do, Don't You?"
that moved him more than any music he had ever heard,
even a blues. It made him want to write church music that
would give others the same heart-shaking experience he
had known. But he had to earn a living, and he took a job
with a band. Later he organized a band for Ma Rainey
and went on tour with her company. Her Rabbit Foot

Minstrels followed the South's black entertainment cir-
cuit. That meant from cotton plantations to sugar fields to
turpentine distilleries—wherever blacks labored. During
this time Dorsey became known as Georgia Tom, the blues
pianist and composer. It was not until 1932 that he returned to the church and the writing of sacred songs. He
wrote some four hundred of them in the course of his
career. Most famous is "Precious Lord Take My Hand"
which became the Reverend Martin Luther King's favorite.

Mahalia listened while Dorsey talked about the bright
future for gospel music. He wanted Mahalia to sing his
new songs. They could lift the spirit and inspire blacks to
carry on the unfinished fight for freedom. But should she
agree to go on the road with Dorsey? She was getting
along in years—twenty-eight now. She had to put something aside for a rainy day. Would this be the way to do
it? Could she spend still more years living out of a suitcase? That was one of the reasons she and Ike had broken
up. He wanted a wife in the home, not on the road.

Mahalia admired Dorsey. Like herself, he wasn't
ashamed to admit he had been born in the South. Nor was
he ashamed of his gospel music, the music some middle-
class blacks derided as "cotton-picking" songs, calling
gospel singers "nappy-headed shouters."

Mahalia didn't want to be selfish. But she had to
consider her Chicago income as against what she might
make on the road with Dorsey. She was earning ten dollars
a week singing at funerals. Occasionally she earned as

much as fifty dollars a week from concerts, and the free-will offerings added something on top. Now and then she got twenty-five dollars for cutting a record.

Finally she said yes. "But I don't want to stay away from Chicago too long. I'm planning to go into business —open a beauty parlor."

Dorsey nodded.

"We'll get back to Chicago often enough for you to do what you like," he said.

What she didn't tell Dorsey was that she wanted to get out of Chicago. The town wasn't big enough for Ike and herself. It was too painful, being in the same place, expecting him to call her and tell her that he was coming back. Then, on the other hand, if he called and found her away, he might ask around and find out she was touring with Dorsey and come looking for her. Maybe they'd try again?

To drive the car Dorsey hired Bob Jones, an old gospel singer who had lost his voice. The only trouble with Bob was that he would doze off sometimes while driving and lose the way. The three of them headed south from Chicago early on a Friday morning to give an evening program in a Baptist church in Springfield, Illinois. Their gas tank was full. They also carried an emergency supply of gas and oil in case they ran out and a white filling-station attendant chose not to sell them fuel. That sometimes happened to blacks in this part of the country. Mahalia had prepared sandwiches and coffee, so they wouldn't have to go to the rear of restaurants to buy food.

Dorsey had been over this road many times with circuses and jazz bands or accompanying Ma Rainey or with his "Evenings with Dorsey." For a while he talked of the past. Then he began telling Mahalia how she should sing "If You See My Savior, Tell Him That You Saw Me."

Mahalia smiled sweetly and told Dorsey she would sing the song the way she wanted to. She had to wait till the moment before she started singing to find out how she felt she should sing.

Dorsey groaned and shook his head. Hadn't he composed songs greatly respected by blacks? And written for successful white orchestra leaders and singers too? He reminded Mahalia that he knew music from A to Z. But as they came closer to Springfield, they stopped arguing. They had more important business to take care of. First of all, they had to overcome the objections of many ministers to gospel songs and gospel singers. They must persuade black middle-class congregations to listen and give gospel music a chance. But to reach them, they had first to calm the fears of black ministers.

It came down to this—if a minister let a gospel singer in his church, that gospel singer had the means to take over the spiritual leadership of the church. She could sing one song and set a church on fire with more spirited rejoicing than a preacher could with a two-hour sermon. And most gospel singers were, after all, women! Could a preacher stand to one side while a woman took over the leadership of his flock?

Another thing that put preachers off was the holy

dancing. Sometimes a gospel song made people happy enough to cut a few steps right inside church. Way back, Andrew Bryan, the founder of the black Baptist church, had to discourage blacks who wanted to dance in the church as they had danced at religious ceremonies in Africa.

So from the early days of the black church in America, inspired members learned to dance "silently," and the preacher allowed them to, as long as they did not cross their feet. Now, with gospel music, dancing was breaking out again, and some ministers didn't like it. This was bringing jazz into the church. It wasn't dignified.

When they came to the little Baptist church in Springfield where Mahalia was to sing, she realized it was too poor to afford even a church mouse. The floor sagged under her weight. Through the cracks in it, she could see the basement below. No matter.

They began their program. Dorsey played the piano and Mahalia sang. After a moment Dorsey stopped to remind Mahalia he *was* playing one of his own compositions. He didn't like the way she was rearranging it, bending his notes, giving his lyrics her own phrasing. But he had to admire the young woman. Big, forceful, fiery, overpowering with her talent and presence, she was a real stretch-out singer, breaking all the rules, changing the melody and meter as the spirit dictated. Singing to that mysterious inner beat that would present difficulties to any musician who tried to accompany her.

When Dorsey and Mahalia finished, the audience's

"Thank you Jesus," "Thank you Jesus," "Thank you Jesus," took a long time to end.

In the back of the church, Bob checked the cash receipts. Dorsey and Mahalia would get 40 percent. The church took 60. Bob's other duties were to sound out officials of the church and find out if they wished to send a gospel choir to Chicago later to take part in Dorsey's gospel choir-training program. He also handled the sale of Dorsey's songs and made arrangements for them to return the following year for another gospel program. Bob had traveled with Dorsey from the days when the converted jazz musician played for Ma Rainey and the unsaved. One of his last chores was to find out the best route to their next stop.

The gospel pioneers stayed long enough after the program to eat supper. That was why they were called "fish-and-bread" singers. "We sang for our supper as well as for the Lord," Mahalia said. Then on to Cairo, Illinois, and from there to Memphis, and on down to Birmingham. They traveled over bumpy dirt roads, and Mahalia saw blacks working the vast stretches of land. They drove through company-store country where from one crop to another the people lived on credit from the grocer. It was a land where the roof over these people's heads was rented to them by the same man who sold them the meat, molasses, and cornmeal on credit.

Down here among these people Mahalia felt she had come back to her source, and it renewed her. Here in the unhurried South she was one with her people.

While they traveled, Dorsey began writing songs especially tailored to fit Mahalia's style. As she sang the songs written for her, she found that people began following her from town to town, from church to church. And she saw it pleased Dorsey when his songs, his soloists, his gospel music, were treasured by audiences above the gospel music of his competitors.

Birmingham was established as the gospel capital of America. But nearby Bessemer tried to take the crown away from Birmingham with a gospel program that featured some of the most popular singers in the land. They called this program "Back to God Day." When it came Mahalia's turn to sing, she saw more people than she had ever before sung for. Fifty thousand! A crowd made up of blacks and whites, separated; some standing, others sitting in their shabby wagons, behind their tired horses and mules, they were separated but equal in their love of gospel songs.

This time she could not sing with her eyes shut, for Dorsey had scores of new compositions for her to try. He handed them to her, one by one, and she read the words and sang. There were twenty of them before she finished, and he let her sing them her own way. The people who had come hundreds of miles to hear her went wild, some of them fainting, falling out, doing holy dances all over the place.

For five years Mahalia traveled with Thomas Dorsey. She sang his songs her own way, fighting most of the suggestions he made to "improve" her voice. Some of his advice she did listen to, such as how to "talk up a song" in between verses, how to protect herself from crooked promoters, how to work out contracts for sharing in royalties from her recordings. And how to appraise her audience: "When I enter a meeting I don't know what I'm going to sing. I walk in, I get the vibrations of the people in the place, and then the song comes," she said.

But five years of bouncing over the country in autos and living out of a suitcase were enough. She was tired of one-night stands. She was thirty-three now. It was time to settle down in Chicago. Time to find a husband, and have a family if the good Lord was willing.

Now and then she had interrupted her travels to return to Chicago to take lessons in beauty culture and flower arranging. Her touring over, she did not come home without the means to make a go of it in business. She opened Mahalia's Beauty Parlor, and when she saw that prosper, she started another business—Mahalia's House of Flowers.

Blacks bought flowers from her for weddings, parties, and funerals so that they could engage her to sing at their affairs. She could have sold them weeds provided her voice went with the weeds. She sold a lot of flowers because she knew a large number of ministers and undertakers who were always trying different ways to get her to sing for them. As for her beauty shop, she knew all the gospel singers in Chicago. They came to get their hair washed and set.

Mahalia became a success in business. She bought

property with her profits. First came an apartment house, so she'd have a place all to herself where she could sing as loudly as she pleased. On weekends she laid aside the cares of her shops and her real estate, and traveled to the ghettos of Detroit, Newark, Philadelphia, and New York —where blacks wanted her to sing the old songs of faith the way they had heard them sung in cotton fields, under revival tents, and at churches like Mount Moriah. To these blacks her songs were like letters from folks back home.

⊰ 14 ⊱

"Move On Up a Little Higher"

A lot of water spilled over the dam before Mahalia made
the record in 1946 that won her national fame and earned
her a fortune.

She had learned to sing "My Country 'Tis of Thee"
and to pledge allegiance to the American flag in a Jim
Crow school. She had nursed and protected white children
who had grown up and passed her in the street without
so much as a smile of recognition. She had waited in line
at Jim Crow windows to buy humiliation at the going
price. Gone to the rear of restaurants for a carry-out
sandwich and cold coffee in a leaky cup. Drunk bitter
water from a FOR COLORED fountain. Straightened black
women's kinky hair because if "we smooth the moss, look

more like whitey, maybe they'll see we're trying to shape up." Been cold and hungry in a tenement. Sung and wept at funerals for the poor. Broken her heart over a gambling man. Seen black men treated like second-class citizens in the armed forces of a country fighting a world war for freedom.

She had ranged up and down America by bus, car, and train, making one-night stands in churches whose names are a roll call of the faithful: Shiloh Baptist, Mount Zion, First, Second, Refuge, Triedstone, Bethel, and Salem. Singing for the fried chicken, potato salad, the collar buttons in the free-will offering and for the glory of her God. Looking for love and another husband.

When Mahalia made her big record—she was thirty-five at the time—she had settled down without bitterness on her side of the color line. She had gone all the way from Water Street to the South Side. There was enough in the bank for her to sing when she wanted to and the way that she chose. She was her own woman.

The true story of the song "Move On Up a Little Higher" and how it came to be recorded may never be known. It's part of the legend surrounding Mahalia Jackson. According to one account, a black gospel composer, the Reverend W. Herbert Brewster, a magnificent competitor of Dorsey, wrote the song. But Mahalia said she had been singing the song since she was a child, long before Brewster composed it. One day she was warming up her voice, singing the words of the song in a studio, when Bess Berman of Apollo Records heard her:

One of these mornings I'm going to lay down my
* cross and get my crown.*
As soon as my feet strike Zion, I'm going to lay down
* my heavy burden*
I'm gonna put on my robes in glory and move on up
* a little higher. . . .*

Bess Berman liked the way Mahalia sang the song and asked her to make a recording right then and there. She did—at least that's one version of the story.

Later, when Studs Terkel invited her to sing on the WFMT Hi-Fi program in Chicago, Mahalia sang these words:

The secret of life, I am told is,
Keep on moving.
You got to have heart, You got to take hold,
Keep on moving.
Heaven and help are on their way.
Walk together, children,
Take my hand. Today is the day.
Only love can make it go.
Keep on walking, Keep on moving. . . .

In another version, Mahalia said that one day in 1946 as she was preparing for a concert in the Golden Gate Ballroom, to limber up her voice, she sang an old spiritual, "Move On Up a Little Higher."

Johnny Meyers, then a promoter of gospel songs, came by and happened to hear her. "What's that you're singing, Mahalia?" he asked.

"Why it's just an old song," she said. "I've always sung it—since I was a little child down in New Orleans."

"You sing it just right," he said. "Why don't you make a record of it?"

Whichever way it happened, when Bess Berman put the record on sale, people stood in line at record stores the way they had for Bessie Smith's records in the early twenties. One hundred thousand of the recording were sold overnight. Two hundred thousand, a million, on and on the sales soared. Demands for Mahalia's appearances poured in. She bought a Cadillac for her tours. It was a big Cadillac, so that when she sang in cities where hotel accommodations were For Whites Only, she'd have a place to sleep. Big enough too to store food in, so she wouldn't have to go to the rear door of a Jim Crow restaurant when she was hungry. The Cadillac helped her forget the humiliation she suffered riding in Jim Crow railway coaches or at the back of buses.

When she stopped to autograph her record for her fans they told her how much her singing meant to them. Some said the song encouraged them to believe that they could succeed, as she had. They said the song roused the downtrodden and made them try harder.

The song was like the overture for the civil rights struggle of the fifties and sixties. It opened the golden age of gospel music. It made it big business. It earned for Mahalia the title of gospel queen.

The recording of "Move On Up" sold over two million copies. Music critics claimed that one million people bought Mahalia's records because they thought she was a blues singer, and the other million because they thought it was black religious music at its finest.

Her share of profits from the big record was a hundred thousand dollars. It came as a surprise, even though Mahalia and Bess argued for the next few years over just how much Mahalia was entitled to. One day, on her way back from making a big deposit at her bank, she stopped at a toy shop. She asked the clerk for the biggest doll in the store. As a child there had never been enough to buy a single toy. She carried the doll home with her, feeling foolish because Christmas was a long way off.

⋖ 15 ⋗

Gospel Queen

Many letters from strangers came to Mahalia now that millions had bought her record and she had become gospel queen. Many were letters from people who wrote to tell her how to spend—and share—her money with them. Lots of people with the last name of Jackson who thought they were related to her wrote to say they were on their way to Chicago to help her celebrate her fame and divide her fortune. There were other letters from inventors, promoters of get-rich-quick schemes, and prospective bridegrooms. All they needed to succeed was her money.

She had to sift the propositions flooding in on her by mail and telephone. She was a simple woman with a big heart. But first things first. She had to settle matters with

the gospel-singing women she had vied with over the years
to find out who was the best. Word had reached her that
her gospel-singing "friends" suspected her of having something extra special going for her all the time. These were
the same ones who lied about her when she was selling
Ike's cosmetics and said her roots and herbs would harm
people.

Later, when she appeared on a program with a number of gospel singers, she chose to sing "How I Got Over"
to tell "these jealous-hearted women" the truth. She took
time in between verses—the way Dorsey had taught her
to take time to talk up a song. She held up her work-
roughened hands and said: "You got to work with your
hands, sisters. All artists should work with their hands.
How can you sing 'Amazing Grace' without using your
hands? My hands demonstrate what I feel inside. What
I've been through. My feet, my hands. I throw my whole
body into what God wants me to sing. My mind and my
voice by themselves are not enough. You've got to put your
soul into it. That's how I got over."

There were tears in her eyes when she finished. She
hoped they had gotten the message. But they hadn't, and
she knew they'd go on lying about her. They'd keep calling
her a handkerchief-headed Aunt Jemima who was willing
to sell her own people down the river if it meant some
gain for her, and then come round asking for a handout
when things got tough. But she'd give them money and
pray for their smallness. No, she hadn't convinced them
that she did not have powerful white friends on the other

side of the color line helping her. After all, getting out of the ghetto, getting free from Jim Crow, was too much like breaking out of a prison for any black in her right mind to believe she had made it all by herself.

At one time it did look as if God had given her the green light.

For just when she most needed an accompanist, Mildred Falls appeared. Mahalia didn't need too much music to back her voice. She'd been singing all by herself for a long time. A pianist helped, if that pianist knew Mahalia was calling the tune, knew how Mahalia felt about what she was to sing at the moment. Happily Mildred Falls knew just what Mahalia wanted. And Mildred could write songs, too. Just for Mahalia. She began playing for Mahalia and stayed with her to the end.

A little later, when Mahalia needed someone to talk with, someone she could trust to help her make the most of her break, along came the Chicagoan Studs Terkel. Author, critic, actor, radio and television personality, expert on both folk music and jazz, Terkel invited Mahalia to appear on one of his programs on Station WFMT. Convinced that Mahalia was a natural performer for television, he featured her on his programs till her wide appeal was recognized and she got her own TV show. Her talks with Terkel helped Mahalia to figure out what to do in the vast new horizon her big record opened out for her.

Another break came for Mahalia through the brilliant black disc jockey and gospel promoter Joe Bostic. Bostic had arranged concerts for Mahalia in Harlem before she

cut her big record. He introduced Mahalia to Marshall
Stearns, the white author of *The Story of Jazz,* and founder
and director of the Institute of Jazz Studies. He had spent
a lifetime studying Afro-American music. Together with
music scholars from places like the Juilliard School of
Music and Columbia he was holding a symposium on the
origins of jazz at Music Inn in Lenox, Massachusetts.

When Stearns invited Mahalia to sing at Music Inn,
she and Mildred Falls got into the Cadillac and drove to
Massachusetts. As they rolled along a road bordered by
estates with magnificent formal gardens, Mahalia slowed
down so they could see the houses the rich lived in. One
of these days she was going to buy herself a home, said
Mahalia. Somewhere in Chicago away from the stockyards
and the elevated, the congestion and dirt of the South
Side. She had the money for it tucked away in the bank.

The first evening, after dinner, Stearns introduced
Mahalia and Mildred to the music experts. There were, in
addition to the American scholars, visitors from music
conservatories abroad. Among them were men and women
who had spent years studying the history of black music
and had published books about it. There were writers from
major American and English magazines, composers, and
jazz and blues buffs who couldn't get enough of hearing
the music and talking about it. Before she and Mildred
could put the right names to the right faces, Stearns led
them to the big music room.

Mildred sat down at the piano and looked at Mahalia
who told her to play "Didn't It Rain, Lord!" When she

finished, the applause was so deafening the only way she got them quiet was to sing: "Jesus, Savior, Pilot Me." And finally, "I'm Going to Move On Up a Little Higher."

Then the questions came: Who had taught her to sing? Where had she developed such tonal shading and rhythm? Did she know that she was "lining-out"?

Mahalia told them that the Baptist church choir was her first school, that she had graduated to gospel singing on Chicago's South Side, and traveled with Dorsey, making the rounds of gospel tents in one-night stands. But the experts wouldn't have it that way. They talked about how West Coast Africans, coming to America in the first half of the eighteenth century, had learned the hymns of Dr. Isaac Watts, the nonconformist British clergyman. Because they could not read, and were singing in a new language, they used the method called lining-out, in which one singer would sing a line and the congregation would repeat it after him. Another reason for lining-out, besides being unable to read, was the lack of books to read from. Mahalia told them both conditions existed in the church she sang in when she was five and she had been "singing Dr. Watts" ever since. The discussion went on for a week, Mahalia singing, Mildred Falls playing, and the experts asking questions and arguing among themselves.

Then on the last day Mahalia told the people at Music Inn what she thought of their analyzing gospel till all the bounce had been taken out of her: "When you try to write down the exact note for the exact sound, for the exact beat, *you lose it.* That's what happened to the black spirituals the Fisk Jubilee Singers sang. They kept writing down the notes and watering down these black spirituals till they began to sound like Tin Pan Alley garbage.

"As for my style of gospel singing, it comes from the bottom of my heart. And I feel I'm a failure unless my audience gets filled with the joyful spirit and gets out of their seats and dances in the aisles. I mean doing the holy dance like they did in the Holiness churches when I was a kid. Take the way I sing 'When the Saints Go Marching In.' The way the songwriters put it on paper, I'm supposed to sing the phrase four times. But since I don't know how to read music, I'm free. So when I sing it, I may feel like singing it twelve times, and then come right to the end with the right bounce and the right beat."

"If you sing 'When the Saints Go Marching In,' I promise to do a holy dance when the spirit moves me," said Stearns. Mahalia sang, and Stearns rose and began clapping. And before Mahalia came to the end of her song, she was leading Stearns and all the experts in a joyful mood like the brass band in New Orleans back from "cutting the body loose."

The experts did agree on one thing. Mahalia had preserved black singing. She had not let European music destroy her Afro-American roots. Despite all the people who wanted her to sing like whites, Mahalia had kept the faith in black music. And in doing so, she had enriched the treasury of black American song.

⊷ 16 ⊷

Carnegie Hall

The first thing Mahalia thought she would do when she got back to Chicago from Music Inn was to find that dream home and buy it. She had hardly finished unpacking when Joe Bostic was on the phone. Everybody in New York wanted to hear her sing. Would she come and give a concert in New York? Sure. New York meant Harlem or one of the big Baptist churches in Brooklyn where Bostic lived. No, he meant a concert in Carnegie Hall! You mean the Carnegie Hall on Fifty-seventh Street where the greatest orchestras and singers in the world performed? The very same Carnegie Hall! He had to be out of his mind. That's what was wrong with young blacks. They didn't know where to stop.

"I'm not afraid to play in Carnegie Hall," said Mildred.

"Hush, Mildred. One fool at a time," said Mahalia while she listened to Bostic tell her that the session at Music Inn had started all the experts talking about her. Now more of them wanted to hear her voice. Besides, he said, you feel you're somebody in Chicago, but unless you come to New York and get measured by the critics there, you might just as well be a midget. New York is where they measure you and tell the rest of the world you're ten feet tall. New York has the critics, the magazines, and newspapers to tell the world Mahalia is truly ten feet tall. And after New York you can go anywhere, and the people, having heard you've conquered the big town, will acclaim you as a winner.

But there was no guarantee she would succeed in Carnegie Hall. Worse, there was a chance she might fail there and lose the following it had taken her twenty-five years to build. Would these high-class people who came to Carnegie Hall understand her songs?

"God moves in a mysterious way His wonders to perform," said Bostic. Who knows what may come out of this concert? Maybe an even wider acceptance of gospel singing from whites? Maybe gospel will break down the color line? This convinced Mahalia. She agreed to give the concert.

Coming into Carnegie Hall on that evening—it was October 4, 1950—Mahalia saw thousands of white and black people milling around the entrance. They pushed and crowded to get to the box office to buy standing-room tickets. Bostic told her blacks had come from as far away as Pittsburgh and Raleigh, North Carolina. They were going to have to seat people on the stage; there'd be space only for the piano, Mildred, and herself. After Bostic left, Mahalia prayed that she wouldn't let her people down. She went out on stage dressed in a flowing powder-blue gown. A hush came over the hall as she and Mildred took their places in the center of the stage.

Mahalia looked out over the audience. She saw the white-clad nurses stationed round the hall to aid those who became emotionally overwrought from the gospel songs. She saw tier after tier of faces, all with that expectant look: "We are waiting to see why so much fuss is being made over you." She'd be the laughing stock of Chicago and New Orleans if her voice failed her. She looked down and felt like a peacock with colorful plumage and ugly feet. Mildred reassured her. From far away, it seemed, she heard Mildred strike the piano keys. Steadfast and faithful Mildred, who could almost read her mind when it came to playing for her the way she wanted the music played.

Mahalia closed her eyes and went back in time to the last Sunday she sang in Mount Moriah Baptist Church. And softly she began "Sometimes I Feel Like a Motherless Child." She sang it as though putting a baby to sleep in his cradle. Then she sang "If You Want to Go to Heaven—

Shout." It was not so much a concert as a shared experience welling up from deep inside her. She took people back in time to their roots, to their longing for peace.

At one point a tall black woman rose from her seat. She raised both arms rigidly to heaven. People tried to restrain her. She got away and came dancing down the aisle toward Mahalia, exclaiming each step of the way: "How good it is, Sweet Jesus!" When a white-clad nurse rescued her, others took to holy dancing, clapping their hands, and crying for joy. That's when Carnegie Hall began to rock. The more the audience clapped and cried out for her songs, the more Mahalia sang till she was carried away and got down on her knees. Then Mildred warned her. After all they *were* on New York's Fifty-seventh Street. Mahalia got up from off her knees and said, "Now we do best remember we're in Carnegie Hall, and if we cut up too much, they might put us out."

Mahalia's heart was pleased. The old black magic had reached Carnegie Hall. The gospel music that can make a somebody out of everybody had done it even on Fifty-seventh Street.

✥ 17 ✥

Golden Harvest

By 1950 Mahalia was earning fifty thousand dollars a year
from her voice. She could hardly believe it. She had never
dreamed this was possible. Besides her income from concert tours, radio, television, and recordings, she was getting huge offers from nightclub owners and jazz band
leaders. These she turned down, explaining that she had
made a vow in 1934 never to sing where whisky was sold.
The nightclubs promised her they would not serve whisky
while she sang. Still she refused.

Mahalia found out that once she became a leader
she became a plainly marked target. When the whisky
sellers couldn't get Mahalia, they hired other gospel singers—some black, some white. To cash in on the golden

period of gospel, which Mahalia and other dedicated singers had inaugurated, operators opened gospel night-clubs. Their doormen were dressed in white choir robes. Scantily dressed girls wearing wings sold whisky by the glass while they sang gospel songs. It angered church leaders. "How," a black bishop asked, "can we expect the white race to respect our spirituals when we do not re-spect them ourselves? These songs, which inspired the idea of freedom for blacks, have been desecrated by some singers. They lose their deep religious import and their significance in black culture the way they are being used in nightclubs. They should be sacred."

Mahalia continued to serve God. She lived simply, saving her money because "success was too good to last." She could never forget the bad times; it felt safer to have cash for the rainy days that were bound to come. Her only luxury was the Cadillac she lived in when touring sections of America where a black with a million dollars did not have enough to buy an unsegregated glass of water.

It made for emotional hardship—living inside the ghetto one day and crossing the next day to whitey's turf. She put it this way: "It's not that I think I'm a special black. Not at all. I don't expect to be treated better than any other black. It's just when I move back and forth between the white and black worlds every day, the stupidity and cruelty of Jim Crow hurts. It hits you so hard you don't know whether to explode with anger or stay on your knees praying for understanding, praying for whites and blacks to get hatred out of their hearts so they can get on with the business of living. While on the concert stage or in the TV studio white people say they love me. On the street they ignore me."

In the midst of her golden harvest she did not forget the faithful people who had encouraged her when she earned $1.50 a day. Shortly after she returned to Chicago from the Carnegie Hall triumph Mahalia planned a surprise for her old friends. Her plan included the gospel singers with whom she used to share the collar buttons in the free-will offerings. Women like Bessie Griffin, an old New Orleans friend, who many blacks claimed could outsing Mahalia out of one corner of her mouth but hadn't gotten the breaks. And Marie Knight, and the Dixie Hummingbird Quartet. Mahalia rented the Chicago Coliseum for her surprise and announced the event as a celebration for her twenty-six years in gospel. Admission was $.75 or $2.50. The proceeds were shared by all the singers except Mahalia. A loud speaker piped the singing into the streets for those who could not afford to pay. The concert was a great success. People danced in the streets.

Then Mahalia gave a series of concerts to raise money for Greater Salem Baptist, her church. It was used to build an extension to the recreation room and to send children from the South Side's hot streets to summer camp. She put aside money to take care of needy members of her own family, enlarged now by members of her father's second family, and the aunts, uncles, and cousins who had come to Chicago.

In 1952, television provided Mahalia with the chance to sing for a vast new audience. Ed Sullivan, who conducted television's most popular program, invited her to appear on Sunday night, January 20. Ed Sullivan's program would put Mahalia into the living rooms of whites and blacks—twenty million owners of television sets— electronic integration!

When Mahalia got to the studio to tape her part in the CBS show she had misgivings. She shook her head and looked at Mildred. Most upsetting was that there was not one black employee to be seen. Then she heard the studio musicians who would accompany her—all white too. She listened to find if these men had the right feeling for black gospel music. They were handcuffed to their sheet music. They did not understand her kind of improvisation. Nor could she explain this something deep inside her, that shaped the time and the tone of her singing. How could any accompanist but Mildred Falls play for her?

The only way to keep her own style of singing from being ruined by the white musicians was to get organ music to back her. But Mr. Sullivan did not want an organ on his program. She didn't care what Mr. Sullivan didn't want. She'd have an organ, or she wouldn't sing. A studio employee led Mahalia to Sullivan's dressing-room door.

She knocked.

"Come in," barked Sullivan.

She opened the door. There stood Sullivan in his underwear. Mahalia explained that she needed an organ to accompany her. Sullivan slipped into a dressing robe. "All right, you may have one," he said.

That night Mahalia added a gospel chapter to television's early history. And won her fight to keep singing Sister Mahalia's own sweet way. The letters that poured in from new converts to gospel singing convinced CBS's record department to sign her to make records exclusively for them.

Mahalia did not get back to Chicago to go home hunting for some months. Following her success on television, she learned that the French Academy of Music had honored her recording of "I Can Put My Trust in Jesus" with an award. Would she come to France to receive it? Her fans in Europe made it plain that if she came to France she should give them a chance to hear her. England, Holland, Belgium, Denmark—they all wanted Mahalia.

Mahalia hated to travel. She was afraid to fly. Ships made her ill. But at the age of forty-one, she put aside her fears and set out to bring gospel music to Europe.

Her first concert in London was a disaster. It was hard to tell which was the more disappointed—Mahalia or the English. She couldn't turn them on. After she sang, they sat on their hands. What made it all the more disappointing for Mahalia was that the English knew the language she was singing.

When she sang for the Danes in Copenhagen, their warm reception made up for the English. The Danes wept when she sang. The day after her concert in Copenhagen, hundreds of school children bearing flowers gathered at her hotel to honor her. In return Mahalia made a record—"Silent Night"—for a Danish company. Overnight fifty thousand Danes bought it.

By the time her tour reached France, she had to have a small army of police to guard her from admiring fans. Then in Bordeaux, on stage in the middle of a song, she fainted and had to be rushed to a hospital. The doctors put it to her bluntly. "If you want to live you'll have to give up singing. You're a very sick woman." They thought she needed surgery. Mahalia shook her head. Weak and weary, she insisted on being flown back to Chicago. If she was that ill, she wanted to take her chance of recovery back home.

❦ 18 ❧

"Walk Together, Children"

In the Billings General Hospital in Chicago, Mahalia lingered between life and death. After a serious operation she lost 90 pounds. As she slowly recovered, she wondered if there were enough spunk left in her remaining 110 pounds for her to sing again. She talked to her doctors. They recommended a long period of rest. What about the singing? The doctors said no. She talked with her spiritual advisor for thirty years, the Reverend Leon Jenkins of Greater Salem Baptist Church. "All healing is divine," he said, urging her to follow her doctors' advice.

But Mahalia did not have time to rest. She couldn't stand illness. She had to keep her hand at something. She left the hospital humming snatches of her old fighting song, "Move On Up a Little Higher." And to celebrate her escape from death, she sang gospel songs to save wayward souls at a one-week revival at Greater Salem. She told the congregation that God had let her live. She was going to sing for His glory till the end.

She gained strength and began singing on her own local television show. Her majestic voice took on new richness. The letters from her fans poured in. Chicago's Poles, Czechs, Yugoslavs, Ukrainians, Germans, Scandinavians, Irish, Italians, Jews, as well as blacks, wrote to Mahalia as an old friend. Her show's Jewish producer persuaded her to sing songs dear to his people. Not to be outdone, her Irish sponsor got her to sing his people's songs. She banked the income from the program for a school she planned to open for young people who wanted an education in music and were too poor to pay tuition.

Then one day Mahalia asked the television people why they didn't put her show on a national hookup. "We'd love to, Mahalia, but we can't do it. You're all right up North here in Chicago, but there isn't a sponsor who sells his product down South that would take a chance on having a black singer on the program." What happened later showed how wrong "the experts" were. The half-hour Chicago show was purchased by a distributor and sold to stations throughout the country.

It was after she started looking for a new home to purchase that Mahalia's kitchen radio brought her news of the sweeping decision by the United States Supreme Court outlawing racial segregation in public schools. The "separate but equal" doctrine the Court had upheld in 1896 when Homer Plessy lost his case was set aside on May 17, 1954. Now the Supreme Court said, *"We conclude that in the field of public education the doctrine of separate but equal has no place. . . ."*

Mahalia's mind went back to New Orleans when she was a child. Dare she believe that all that stupid Jim Crow had come to an end? Or would this be another bitter disappointment? Blacks had come up from the South to Chicago filled with hope of better days only to have the Great Depression throw them out of their jobs. Last to be hired, first to be fired. Mahalia was cautious that day in her kitchen while she listened to the news report. This wasn't the first time America had offered blacks hope. The Supreme Court might declare Jim Crow unconstitutional, but could the Court enforce its own decision? Would the government stand behind it?

She wondered if white and black children would really go to school together now. Or would that decision harden the color line separating black from white? Only time would tell. But this was no time to fear the worst. Mahalia began rejoicing in the knowledge that at last Homer Plessy and the countless blacks who had been beaten, mobbed, and lynched in their fight for equal rights had brought about this victory. She took a red crayon and circled the date on the calendar.

But soon after, the white South reacted as Mahalia had feared. White Citizens' Councils sprang up, organized to deny blacks the fruits of the Supreme Court's decision. Politicians swore they would defy the Constitution. They vowed to keep Jim Crow at all costs. Despite these early signs of resistance to the law, blacks were hopeful. The law was at last on their side. Maybe this time white supremacy would be destroyed once and for all.

Joining in the jubilation, Mahalia kept on searching for a home to buy. She got in her car and drove from neighborhood to neighborhood. Wherever she saw a "For Sale" sign, she stopped and asked the price. The owner would slam the door in her face without answering her question, or say he had changed his mind—the property was no longer for sale.

After Mahalia had covered Chicago's suburbs without success, she went to a real estate agent. He made use of her public reputation, advertising for someone to sell a home to Mahalia Jackson, the Gospel Queen. A white dentist, a fan of Mahalia's, replied. "I'll be proud to sell my house to Mahalia," he said.

That wasn't the way his neighbors felt. When they learned she had bought the dentist's seventy thousand dollar home—an eight-room, red brick, ranch-style house with picture window and California patio—they were furious. A Catholic priest went about the all-white neighborhood imploring his parishioners to give Mahalia a chance.

Some of the neighbors believed that if they let Mahalia live in peace, other black families would move in too. Rumors spread that Mahalia had ten children, all school age. And what terrible things would happen to their schools with all those black children in them? With other blacks moving in to join Mahalia, this would cheapen the value of each white person's home. Their seventy thousand dollar homes would become thirty-five thousand dollar properties! They'd lose what they had struggled over the years to pay for. Either Mahalia must go or the whites would have to go!

While her decorators were placing the new furniture and antiques in her new home, the phone began ringing. When she answered, she was called foul names by the caller who then hung up. Then the phone rang again. This time the caller said: "Wait and see what we'll do to you. We're going to blow you away with dynamite. Your God won't save you."

"Look, honey, I'm tired, and all I need is a quiet home to live in," she said. But the caller hung up before hearing Mahalia out. Mahalia searched among the odds and ends she had brought with her and found a little framed quotation. She had carried it with her ever since she moved to Chicago. She hung it in her living room: "Dear Lord in This House You Are Wanted and You Are Welcome."

When phone threats didn't drive her out, her windows were shot out by rifle bullets. She was afraid to turn on the lights at night. She appealed to the police for protection. They guarded her house night and day. But who could live this way? Her friends advised her to move. She began packing room by room, until she came to the quotation she had hung on the wall. No, she would stick it out. God was on the side of right.

But she was afraid to stay. She could not rest either

at home or away from home. When her phone rang, she jumped and answered cautiously, not knowing till she heard the voice whether friend or fanatic was calling.

One day Edward R. Murrow of CBS told her he would bring a camera crew to her home and interview her for his nationally televised "Person to Person" program. Mahalia invited her neighbors' children in for ice cream and cake, to be on the program with her. She said she wanted to show that blacks did not eat little children. Many came. But soon her neighbors began moving away, one by one. Blacks bought the homes. Today the neighborhood is almost entirely populated by black businessmen, doctors, lawyers, entertainers, and their families. The blacks take pride in keeping their properties tidy and in good repair. The sun, trees, grass, and birds remain as they did during the time when whites lived there.

Despite the troubles of home and health, Mahalia's career was on a rising curve. It left her little time to worry. Concert tours took her into the Far West, the Deep South, and the East. Appearances in New York before packed audiences were frequent. Her sessions at Music Inn in Lenox, Massachusetts, became an annual affair. Records she made for CBS sometimes sold over a million each. Her earnings went above one hundred thousand dollars a year. Although her schedule made it hard for her to sing in the little churches, she said: "What people don't realize is that the church is my filling station. I get renewed inspiration there. Often I slip off and go anyway. Sometimes I go to some sanctified storefront church at night and sing with the Holiness people till early morning."

Meanwhile the black struggle for equal rights was moving ahead rapidly. Shortly before Christmas 1955, a black seamstress, Mrs. Rosa Parks, got on the Cleveland Avenue bus in downtown Montgomery, Alabama. She was tired from a long day's work standing on her feet in one of Montgomery's department stores. Her feet were killing her. The back of the bus was crowded so she moved on up to an empty seat just behind the white section. The whites sat in the front of the bus, the blacks in the back. But if a white couldn't find a seat in the white section, he could have a black's seat in the rear. And the black would have to stand up.

More white passengers entered the bus, and the driver ordered Mrs. Parks to go to the back of the bus so that a white man could have her seat. The seamstress was terribly tired. And suddenly she felt this was too much. She'd paid her fare and was entitled to her seat. She kept her seat till the bus driver called a cop. The police took Mrs. Parks to jail. It was the way they had treated Homer Plessy that long-ago day in New Orleans.

There were two young Baptist ministers in Montgomery, Martin Luther King and Ralph Abernathy, who came to Rosa Parks's aid and made her arrest history. The two young ministers and a committee of Montgomery black leaders organized the Montgomery Bus Boycott. The seventeen thousand blacks who used to ride the buses walked to work or shared in car pools, their campaign supported by money sent by people all over the world. "Before, my soul was tired of Jim Crow," said one old black lady. "Now, only my feet are tired because my soul has found pride and peace."

The bus company, the police, the White Citizens' Council, the Ku Klux Klan, tried to break the boycott with everything from lawsuits to violence. King's home was bombed. They dynamited Ralph Abernathy's home too. Black churches, the homes and businesses of suspected leaders of the boycott, were bombed and fired. Ninety black leaders were arrested and thrown in jail and charged with conspiracy. Working blacks lost their jobs. Excessive court costs, fines, bails, almost emptied the boycotters' treasury. Money was sorely needed when the two leaders, King and Abernathy, met Mahalia in Denver, at the National Baptist Convention in 1956. She had been invited to sing before the thousands of delegates who represented a membership of over five million blacks.

What she did not know was that after her singing she was to be elected treasurer of the body and named chief of their soloists' department. It would be her job to help train soloists throughout the Baptist realm in the proper singing of church music. It meant her kind of music was no longer barred from the big Baptist churches. At last she had been accepted.

At the convention Mahalia listened attentively to the pleas of the Reverends King and Abernathy. They wanted her to sing in Montgomery to raise money to pay bail, fines, court costs, and lawyers. It would help save their bus boycott. But, Dr. King warned Mahalia, your life will be in danger if you consent to come.

I'll come, she said. I'll sing my gospel songs to help win our rights.

Soon after, Mahalia and Mildred drove out of Chicago to join forces with the Montgomery Bus Boycott. As usual, Mahalia's feet hurt. She took off her shoes and slipped on her Indian moccasins. She settled her two hundred pounds in a comfortable position in the car's front seat and warned the driver to take it easy. She did not like to ride in the back seat. They were going South where highway patrolmen were anxious to arrest black motorists, especially "uppity niggers" riding in the back seat of a Cadillac.

When she was singing on the concert stage or over television, working with white people, they just hugged her and said how great she was. And then when she was walking down the street like an ordinary black, they didn't recognize her, and when she went into a department store in the South, she couldn't buy a sandwich or a Coke. She couldn't even get a cab. And she was just the same Mahalia Jackson they kept saying was so wonderful. It was hard to understand. What made people act like this? Why was this bus boycott necessary? What's wrong that white and black people can't sit down together in peace on a bus long enough to get to where they're going?

But she knew that the Montgomery Bus Boycott was

more complicated than blacks and whites sitting together. It had become more than a mass action on one issue. The blacks had added to their bill of grievances. They wanted the white bus drivers to treat them like human beings. They wanted the bus company to hire black bus drivers on routes passing through black neighborhoods. But they wanted even more. If they won their demands, Montgomery might bring the whole separate but equal structure tumbling down.

When Mahalia and Mildred arrived in Montgomery, the Abernathys gave them their own beds. The Reverend Martin Luther King and his wife came over to help make the travelers feel at home. Mrs. Abernathy cooked one of those down-home dinners that made Mahalia think that the risk to her life in coming to Montgomery was worth it. The minister's wife had made her specialty—spoon bread —with collards cooked with a pinch of soda and sugar, and ham skins on the fat side, and peach cobbler for dessert.

A somber air made it a quiet meal. Members of Alabama's White Citizens' Council had sent the blacks word that they would be out in force to break up the rally Mahalia was to sing for that evening. When King appealed to the local police for help, they replied they did not have enough men to guarantee their safety. The Abernathys put Mahalia's car in a friend's garage to protect it from the mob.

Shortly before the mass meeting, Mahalia, the Kings,

and the Abernathys set out for the rally at the Methodist church. (Baptists and Methodists joining under the roof of one or the other showed what unity the boycott had achieved.)

As they walked to the church, members of the White Citizens' Council drove by hooting at them and calling them filthy names. When they got to the church they saw a thin line of police present to hold back whites who were there to frighten the blacks. But the blacks streamed into the church, paying no attention.

When Mahalia and her party got inside the packed church, the white mob outside surged against the old building. Somehow they were kept out. With sweat streaming from his face, the Reverend Ralph Abernathy opened the meeting. He prayed a long prayer for victory in the bus boycott.

Then committee members gave reports on their work for the bus boycott. Mahalia quietly hummed to herself her fighting song—"Move On Up a Little Higher"—remembering the different times she had warmed her vocal cords for a recital. It was her lucky song too. If only a song could move blacks from the back of the bus to the front!

Finally it was time for her to sing. She rose and looked at Mildred, who sat ready at the piano. Mildred knew what to play. Mahalia began singing "Move On Up a Little Higher." Loudspeakers had been put on the outside of the church so the people in the street who could not find room inside might hear. While Mahalia sang, the segregationists there to disrupt the meeting were silent. Then she sang "Walk Together, Children, Don't You Get Weary."

Now Dr. King rose and began his sermon. Mahalia looked at him. He was only twenty-seven, and a small man physically. He talked quietly at first, so that the people in the back of the church had to strain to hear him. Here was the strength of the ministry, Mahalia thought. His father was an outstanding man of the cloth in Atlanta, Georgia. His grandfather too had been an influential preacher. Blacks should not hate their enemies, Dr. King was saying, not even those who would revile and degrade them. For hate drains off one's energy and we need all our strength to walk till the bus company comes to its senses and treats us justly. Turn the other cheek. Meet violence with nonviolence. The meek shall inherit the earth. . . . A strange feeling came over Mahalia as she listened to King. She thought she had felt like this before. She remembered the vow she had taken when she prayed God to spare her grandfather's life.

Then it came to Mahalia. Dr. King was not a rich man. His church could pay him only a modest salary. He had a wife and a family to support. It would take money, lots of it, to keep this movement going. Couldn't she help Dr. King more than by singing today? Shouldn't she offer the movement part of her savings? That night Mahalia made another solemn vow. She pledged a considerable part of her fortune to support King's drive to bring equal rights to blacks.

After the meeting she and Mildred left Montgomery. The next night the bedroom that she and Mildred had occupied in the Abernathy home was leveled to the ground with dynamite. The Abernathys escaped uninjured.

Proudly, as though they were Jim Crow's pallbearers, Montgomery blacks walked together for over a year while the buses drove through the streets without passengers. While the eyes of the world were on Montgomery, the highest court in the land finally declared that bus segregation within a state was unconstitutional. No catastrophe followed. Black and white riders learned to sit together, peacefully. The buses ran as usual. Buses steered by black drivers, who gained jobs as a result of the boycott, ran like buses anywhere in the world.

The year after the Montgomery victory, the Southern Christian Leadership Conference was organized, and Martin Luther King was elected its president. Congress passed the first Civil Rights Act since Reconstruction days. But laws on the books didn't work automatically. President Eisenhower had to order federal troops into Little Rock to ensure that nine black children could enter Central High School. In Virginia the whites of Prince Edward County chose to shut down the public school system rather than integrate it.

Suddenly four young black students in North Carolina decided to do something that caught the imagination of the whole world. In 1960, they sat down at a lunch counter in Greensboro and ordered cups of coffee. The waiter refused to serve them. He explained that North Carolina law did not allow him to serve blacks in a public eating place—all of which he was sure the young men knew since they were freshmen at North Carolina A & T College.

The students replied that they would sit there till they were served. And they did, until the police came and arrested them. No matter how terribly the police and the mobs treated the young people, they never raised their hands to fight back. They believed in Martin Luther King's preaching of nonviolence and passive resistance.

Within three weeks the sit-in protest spread to fifteen cities in five states of the South. More than a thousand young people were arrested at sit-ins throughout the South. Now there were sit-ins in public libraries, where blacks had been denied the right to borrow books, at swimming pools, beaches, hotel lobbies, movie houses.

The struggle moved north. When the Southern Christian Leadership Conference came to Chicago to fight Jim Crow, Mahalia gave fifty thousand dollars to underwrite its expenses, and Dr. King and his family stayed at her house. She raised funds for the work in Pittsburgh, Detroit, New York, Washington.

Montgomery had been but the beginning of the civil rights revolution. And a new beginning for Mahalia Jackson, too.

❧ 19 ❧

In Europe and the Holy Land

In 1961, soon after she sang "The Star-Spangled Banner" at President John F. Kennedy's inaugural, Mahalia decided to tour Europe again, and this time to visit the Holy Land too. Before she sailed, friends from many cities came to see her off. There were flowers, champagne, and big baskets of fruit for the party. Then it was time for the visitors to leave the ship. With whistles blowing and horns tooting, tugboats pulled the big liner from the dock.

The stewardess prepared the bed. Mahalia was worn out. For two days she couldn't sit up long enough to eat. The stewardess brought her tea and broth. Invitations were sent to her cabin from passengers who wanted her to join them. But Mahalia found she didn't have the energy.

She refused to call the ship's doctor. She didn't want to
hear the bad news that her diabetes had worsened and
that she might have to cancel the trip and go back to Chicago as she had in 1952. This time she meant to succeed.

But finally she did see the doctor. He took her blood
pressure and found it much too low. Then he prescribed
medicine and a diet of steaks, spinach, grapes, and wine.
Mahalia told the doctor she didn't drink. He quoted from
the Bible: "Take a little wine for thy stomach's sake and
thine often infirmities."

" 'Drink no longer water, but use a little wine for thy
stomach's sake and thine often infirmities,' is the way I
was taught that, doctor," said Mahalia.

Easter Sunday, she sang for the ship's Protestant
service. At the end, exhausted, she went back to her cabin
where she sat and looked from her window at the Atlantic.
The sight of the water lulled her to sleep. Mildred woke
her and gave her more notes slipped under the door. Someone wanted her to come to a party for actors bound for
Paris to make a movie. The producer of the Newport Jazz
Festival wanted to take her to dinner. A note from the
ship's radio operator said that London newspapermen
wanted to interview her by way of shore-to-ship telephone.
Not even on the ocean was she free of a phone. She got
up and went to the party for an hour.

Back in her cabin, Mildred went over the songs
Mahalia was to sing on the tour. The programs for London,
Frankfurt, Hamburg, and Berlin. Mildred reminded Ma-
halia that they were also going to shop for crystal goblets

in Hamburg. Then there was the music for Stockholm and Copenhagen. In Paris they were going to shop for lace curtains and linens after the concert. Then they'd have to go back to Germany—Essen and Munich. They'd take it easy in Zurich, and in Rome, where they were to be presented to Pope John XXIII. Then on to Naples for a ship to Alexandria, Egypt. Beirut would be next, then Damascus, Tel Aviv, and Jerusalem. After they had agreed on the programs, Mildred returned to her cabin.

Thoughts of the foreign audiences she was going to sing for made Mahalia break into a cold sweat. She worried again over whether she would be able to carry the meaning of her songs over the walls of language. Would the Germans, the Scandinavians, the French, the Israelis, understand her? She didn't know one word of their languages! Could she make a connection between these people and the country blacks who had fashioned her music?

She remembered when she was a child and her father used to point out the flags waving over the ships that docked on the Mississippi almost in their front yard. England, France, Germany, Italy, Egypt, Denmark, Sweden —she had never dreamed she would travel in all these countries as a concert artist and honored guest.

When the *United States* reached Southampton, reporters and photographers came aboard. After the news conference she had to get ready to tape a television show in London. At the studio, the announcer introduced her by saying, "I advise you not to miss Mahalia. Here is a singer who, whilst adhering strictly to her religious convictions, sings with rhythmical drive and beat that can be rivaled only by the hottest jazz bands. And before which the rhythm of the rock and rollers pales into thin water."

The taping over, there was no time for even a short nap at her hotel. They hustled her off to Albert Hall for the evening's concert. It was five, and there was a lot of work to do.

The hall itself was the first great hurdle to get over. In each place the hall she was to sing in was like a different dragon that could consume and destroy her voice, and reduce Mildred's piano to the tinny sounds of a Jew's harp. She had to test her voice to find out the tricky spots in the walls and ceiling. Technicians had to find these places so they could be closed off with sheets of cloth or wallboard. First she sang to different corners of the hall. Then it was Mildred's turn to find out how the piano sounded in various parts of the stage.

These great European music halls were designed for large orchestras, not for Mahalia's voice, Mildred's lone piano or an organ. Adjustments had to be made for the gospel queen's singing, or even her big voice would have been lost in the very immensity of Albert Hall. When she finally found the best spot for her voice and the piano, Mahalia went to her dressing room. David Haber, her European representative, came to tell her long lines of ticket buyers were forming for her concert. Perhaps this time she might beat the jinx of that first concert on English soil almost a decade ago.

Every seat and all standing room was sold in Albert Hall when Mahalia came out to sing. She chose as her first song, "My Home Over There." She explained that the song reminded her of the Apostle Paul; he who had kept the faith. She said: "I've fought a good fight and I, also, keep my faith." The concert was a great success.

When Mahalia and Mildred came out of the stage door they were met by a surging crowd of fans. Mahalia was knocked to the ground and had to crawl on her hands and knees to a policeman who saved her from autograph seekers. She got to her feet and, though bruised, was too happy to care. The important thing was she had overcome the failure of 1952.

The next day Mahalia read reviews of her concert in the English press. One critic's comments stood out above the others. He said: "Thousands were there but Mahalia sang only to me." That was the way she wanted it.

The night after her concert in Frankfort, Mahalia's German fans gave a party for her. She talked with people who collected her records. They expressed surprise at the difference between her singing in the concert hall and on records. In person her voice was richer and fuller, they said. Mahalia explained how difficult it had been for her to sing with studio accompaniment in America. Most studios where Mahalia cut records were equipped to magnify a small voice. Even worse, some musical directors who presided over the making of her records had added choral groups and orchestra to the record after she had performed her songs. This is called dubbing. The effect was to change the quality of her singing, to make it something less than what it naturally was.

When Mahalia sang in Hamburg's Musikhalle, for a moment she thought she was at Soldiers' Field in Chicago. She had once sung before a hundred thousand in that stadium. Here in Hamburg the audience seemed as huge. The audience patted their feet, they stomped, they clapped as Americans had at Carnegie Hall. In her dressing room she took off her shoes (her feet hurt) and went back to sing all the encores they asked for. Barefoot, she sang as long as they wanted her to.

The reporters were out in force when Mahalia got to Copenhagen. Some of their questions were embarrassing to the proud woman. "How are you as a black treated in America?" She let that one hang while she figured out what they were after. "Can black and white children attend the same public schools in America?" Her heart sank. She wished she had stayed in Chicago. "How many blacks did mobs lynch this year?" "Why do the police turn attack dogs on black children when they try to get a bottle of soda at a public lunch counter?" It was all she could do to hold her temper. She figured that the reporters were hunting for anti-American headlines. She gave her answers through an interpreter.

How was she treated? About like any other black with her income. . . . We've got Martin Luther King, Roy Wilkins, James Farmer, and a lot of brave blacks and decent whites—trying to make things better in America.

Her anger gave way to doubt. Should she tell the reporters how it felt to drink water from a fountain marked FOR COLORED? What a child thought of when he heard of the senseless killing of a black for being black? How angry it had made her father when he met a white man on a sidewalk and had to get off and walk in the gutter?

"All I want to say to these questions is that blacks aren't mad at the decent white Americans. They're mad at segregation. I was born in America. Reared there. Got no other home. Now if they kill me for fighting for freedom I'll be dead in the land of the free. We're gonna walk together. Sing together. And fight together. That's America."

When she got to her hotel room, she fell on the bed and cried.

The next stop was Paris. She found it was like an armed camp. Troops ringed the city and patrolled the streets. Parisians momentarily expected rebellious French troops from Algeria to descend on them. The government was about to give Algeria its independence, and Frenchmen living in Algeria did not want France to free the rich colony. But no attack came. Mahalia filled the concert hall for one of her biggest recitals.

In Zurich, she was an honored guest at a formal dinner in the American Embassy. When she got to Rome, she was presented to His Holiness Pope John XXIII. At Naples she sailed across the Mediterranean to Alexandria to begin her tour of the Middle East.

In the Holy Land, Mahalia reached one of the highest points of her life. Ever since she had joined the church choir at five, Mahalia had been singing about some place in the Holy Land: Jericho, the Dead Sea, Galilee, Bethlehem, Mount Hebron, the Jews escaping across the Red Sea from their Egyptian masters, Jerusalem, Calvary. When she was a child, she had thought she had been singing about places in Heaven, but here these places were, and she said, "Why, it's all still the same! I'm seeing it as Jesus did, with my own eyes. I'm going to walk in Jerusalem, talk in Jerusalem, shout in Jerusalem, pray in Jerusalem.

"And now here I am about to walk the streets where Jesus walked and to pray in Calvary and to see and touch all the things I've always sung about. This is my homecoming."

The night Mahalia came on the stage for her concert in Tel Aviv she wore a white gown and a necklace with a gold cross. Two thousand people—Muslims, Jews, and Christians—waited for her first song. Mahalia prayed that no one would be offended by her choice of songs. She started with "My Home Over There." Then she went on with "The Holy Bible," "Ain't Gonna Study War No More," and "Joshua Fit de Battle of Jericho." When she went off stage, the audience shouted "More! More! More!" Mahalia came back and sang the Joshua song till the walls of the auditorium seemed in danger of coming down. There were more encores till the song she held for her last: "Mahalia's Not Gonna Sing No More."

She sang no more on her way back to the States. The peacefulness of the Holy Land had rested her. A weight seemed to have been lifted off her shoulders. She felt with God's guidance the world's problems might be solved.

When her ship docked in New York, she looked over the railing down on the crowd waiting to welcome the travelers. She saw friends who had come from Philadelphia, Washington, Chicago, to meet her. She saw them before they saw her, and their faces made her glad. It came to her that this must be the way it would be when she died and went to Heaven. There she would meet her mother, the aunts who had reared her, the wonderful ministers and friends who had helped her reach success —they'd all be there to greet her. She was back home. When her time came, Heaven would be like this.

⋗ 20 ⋖

"I Been 'Buked and I Been Scorned"

Red beans and rice simmering with pigs' knuckles, French bread buttered and toasted with garlic, those big red oysters from the Gulf of Mexico, red snapper baked in New Orleans seasoning with plum tomato sauce, smothered crabs and turtles, pepper grass cooked low with streak-o-lean—a feast of these foods was what she'd cook for her friends as soon as she got back to Chicago. When it came right down to it, Mahalia got more enjoyment from cooking for others than from eating now that she had to diet.

But that homecoming feast was hardly over when she was again drawn into the thick of the civil rights struggle. The sit-ins which had started a year ago had toppled segregation at lunch counters in the southern and border states. By now hundreds of places were serving blacks for the first time. The movement had turned to other targets—hotels, movie theaters, playgrounds, parks —and right now to transportation.

Freedom riders—whites and blacks working together in the Congress of Racial Equality—had just gone into Alabama on buses to protest segregation at interstate terminals. White mobs beat them brutally at Birmingham and Anniston. News photos flashed around the world showing the riders stomped on the ground and slashed with chains, their bus burned to a mass of twisted metal.

Immediately a group of black and white students left Atlanta and headed for Montgomery to protest segregation at its bus terminal. Fearing bloodshed, Dr. Martin Luther King called on Attorney General Robert Kennedy to protect these young Americans in their peaceful exercise of their constitutional rights to travel and to speak. Kennedy ordered federal marshals to move in, but before they could reach Montgomery, the students arrived and were attacked by a mob led by Klansmen. They were stoned and slugged, and one black man, not a rider, was drenched in kerosene and set afire.

That day—it was Sunday, May 21, 1961—Dr. King announced he would hold a mass meeting in the evening at the First Baptist Church. He wanted to honor the courageous young freedom riders and to strengthen his parishioners for nonviolent resistance to segregation. Mahalia, who was visiting in the South, got a call from Dr.

King to come and sing in support of the freedom riders.

As soon as the city's racists heard of King's plans, several nearby churches were set ablaze. Firemen refused to douse the flames. The segregationists dynamited the home of a member of the First Baptist Church. Nothing of that sort would change King's mind. As dusk settled on the old capital city of the slaveholding Confederacy, blacks began moving toward the church on Ripley Street. The mob lay in wait. It meant to see that the success of the Montgomery bus boycott five years before was not to be taken by the blacks as the collapse of white supremacy. They would not let the freedom riders force them into giving blacks the same rights as other Americans.

There were other forces fueling the mob's anger. As white southerners, members of the mob prided themselves on "understanding" blacks. They "knew" the local blacks, didn't they? trusted servants, cooks, maids, gardeners, chauffeurs, nurses, rearing and protecting their white children just as Mahalia had. They "knew" *their* blacks didn't want any of this freedom nonsense. They "knew" that terror would frighten *their* blacks away from the Ripley Street church.

And they were angry too because such men as the Reverend King and the Reverend Abernathy, born southerners, were leading this revolt of southern blacks against the old tried and true ways of the South. They'd always said it was northern radicals who came down here and caused trouble with their blacks. So this night they were determined to restore the "good name" of Montgomery. They were determined to stop this church meeting before it started. And they were armed with baseball bats, bricks, cobblestones, kerosene.

They lined the streets leading to the church. Many raced through the town in cars, screaming and cursing at blacks on the sidewalk. Then as the blacks neared the church, they were pelted with eggs, stones, and bricks. They protected themselves as best they could and kept on walking toward the church.

As they entered the church they joined in singing "Love Lifted Me Up!" Mahalia's voice rose above all others. Behind locked doors the fifteen hundred besieged people sang:

Black and white together,
Black and white together,
We shall overcome some day.

The United States marshals arrived. They shot tear gas into the ranks of the mob to disperse them, but the containers fell close by the churchyard, and the gas filtered in through open windows. Many inside the church were made ill. Some ran to the exits. The ushers closed the windows. Now people began fainting from the heat and the excitement.

Mildred Falls struck up "Walk Together Children." Mahalia began singing. While she sang, Dr. King was on the phone with Robert Kennedy: "The mob is moving in on us," said Dr. King. More than the federal marshals was needed. Would the government do something?

"We will stop them," said Kennedy. On another phone the Attorney General talked with the governor of Alabama. He demanded that National Guardsmen be sent in to keep the peace. Slowly the night passed in what must have been the longest church service ever. Then army trucks roared up, and troops in combat dress leaped out. Alabamans all, they did not like this task, but with fixed bayonets they forced the mob out of the area. Daylight broke before the National Guard was able to escort the congregation, the freedom riders, Dr. King, Mahalia, and Mildred to their homes.

After the Alabama crisis, the government moved to wipe out racism in interstate transportation. Segregation was outlawed in all trains, buses, and terminals.

All through the movement in those years, blacks sang their freedom songs. They caught on, said Mahalia, because music speaks to the heart. It says something that can't always be expressed by the spoken word. It was the soul that was reached by music's message, she believed. Even those who didn't believe in God sometimes found Him through music. She knew that. She remembered one young black leader saying, "Without music there could have been no movement."

As for herself, in those early 1960's she felt like a mule put between the shafts to plow the furrow. She sang her way across the country, night after night in a different city. The pace was killing. In 1962 she seemed to fall apart, and her manager, Lew Mindling, cut the tour short and brought her home to Chicago. In the hospital the doctors discovered she had developed heart trouble. So many years on the road had strained her too much. Her concert dates were canceled, and she stayed home all summer to rest. She kept in touch with the civil rights struggle by phone talks with people like Dr. King. "Come down here to Georgia," he said to her once, but she had to reply that if she ended up in jail where most of them were, she'd never live to get out.

Gradually her strength came back. The next year— 1963—marked the centennial of the Emancipation Proclamation. The movement had been chanting "Free by '63" for a long time, but that goal was still somewhere in the future. How patient were blacks supposed to be? Mahalia wondered. It was one hundred years since the slaves had been liberated. But they were still not free and equal. The headlines proved it every day. To enroll two students at the University of Alabama the government had to send in an escort of federal troops. Medgar Evers, the leader of the NAACP in Mississippi, had been murdered in front of his home. People wanting jobs on buildings going up in their own neighborhood in Harlem had to organize mass demonstrations to force the construction unions to let even a few blacks work. Right here in Chicago a quarter of a million students had just boycotted the public schools for a day to protest segregation.

So she was glad to join in the huge Washington demonstration planned for that summer of '63 by A. Philip Randolph, the grand old leader of the fight. It was Randolph who had forced the Fair Employment Practices

bill through when he organized thousands of blacks for a
March on Washington back in 1941. Just the threat of
that demonstration had induced President Roosevelt and
the Congress to act.

Now it was time for another March on Washington
for jobs and freedom. That August day it was lovely
summer weather in the capital. Mahalia had driven in
the night before. By morning the city was packed. Five
hundred special buses and eighteen special trains jammed
with young and old, black and white, had entered the
city from the remotest corners of the continent. People
came too by car, by bicycle, by roller skates, on foot.
Everyone who had taken part in the movement or simply
watched sympathetically from the sidelines felt a powerful desire to be in the center of this demonstration.

Going downtown, Mahalia saw thousands spread out
over the grassy slopes and under the oaks and elms of
the large park stretching between the Washington Monu-
ment and the White House. Everywhere the spirit was
happy, joyous. It was as though the Day of Jubilee had
come at last. She was filled with pride. She felt like
laughing and crying at the same time. Like many of the
other marchers, she took out her camera and snapped
pictures to remember this hour by.

By noon the crowd had grown to 250,000 people. It
was the largest protest rally ever held in Washington.
Now she could hear singing. Knots of people here and
there raised their voices in the old hymns and spirituals

and the new freedom songs, "We Shall Not Be Moved," "We Shall Overcome," "Blowin' in the Wind."

Twenty abreast, the marchers came, heading for the Lincoln Memorial, waving flags and banners and slogans on placards. Mahalia felt they were a mighty host come for deliverance. She thought of those words from the Bible, "And nations shall rise up. . . ." Were her people coming out of the wilderness and crossing over into Canaan?

At the Memorial she took a seat on the platform and listened to the speakers. Before her stretched the vast sea of people. She felt this day had a special meaning for her. Three generations back, her ancestors had been slaves on a Louisiana plantation. In the fifty years since her childhood on the New Orleans levee, she had seen her people move forward. Were they now standing at the gate of the Promised Land?

A feeling of exaltation seized her. She rose to sing. She had worried about the first song for her to sing this day. Martin Luther King had given her the answer—an old spiritual that came out of the way her people felt. She stood before the crowd, and began softly, her voice reaching these thousands and the millions listening and watching on radio and television:

I been 'buked and I been scorned,
I'm gonna tell my Lord
  When I get home,
Just how long you've been treating me wrong.

The joy building within her overflowed and poured out through her magnificent voice. She raised the rhythm to a gospel beat, began clapping her hands and swaying, and the crowd joined in, singing along with her, their hands clapping too, their bodies rocking to her rhythm. For a moment it was a giant revival meeting.

When the applause faded away, Dr. King spoke:

> . . . . I have a dream one day that little black boys and little black girls will be able to join hands with little white boys and girls and walk together as sisters and brothers.
>
> This will be the day when all of God's children will be able to sing with new meaning, "My country 'tis of thee, sweet land of liberty, of thee I sing," and "From every mountainside, let freedom ring."
>
> When we let freedom ring, when we let it ring from every village and every hamlet, from every state and every city, we will be able to speed up that day when all of God's children, black men and white men, Jews and Gentiles, Protestants and Catholics, will be able to join hands and sing in the words of that old Negro spiritual,
>
> *Free at last! Free at last!*
> *Thank God Almighty, we are free at last!*

As Mahalia listened, she realized that Dr. King had altered the words of a song he had known from childhood, ever since he had sat in his father's church. She recalled the other words of the song:

Free at last, free at last, I thank God I'm free at last;
Free at last, free at last, I thank God I'm free at last.
'Way down yonder in the graveyard walk
I thank God I'm free at last.
Me and my Jesus goin' to meet and talk,
I thank God I'm free at last.

Years later she wondered if Dr. King had foreseen the ending of his dream by an assassin's bullet in Memphis, Tennessee, April 4, 1968. Once more she sang for Martin Luther King while the world watched and listened. At the funeral for the slain leader, her voice rose in "Precious Lord Take My Hand." At last he and his Jesus had met and talked.

⊰ 21 ⊱

"If You Never Hear Me Sing No More"

It is the hottest day of July 1969.

Mahalia sits brooding on an outdoor stage in a Harlem park. Some twenty thousand blacks and whites stand before her, waiting for her to sing. Mahalia is trying to "keep the slums cool" by giving free concerts for the public during hot days when rioting is expected. Photographers and television cameramen swarm over the stage shooting pictures of Mahalia.

It has rained earlier in the day. But the sweltering heat has returned to test the crowd's will to stay. The people remain, feasting their eyes on the big handsome woman. A sort of mother to them all. This woman without chick or child. Without husband. (In 1967 her second

148

*marriage, to Minters Galloway, ended after three years.)
The crowd does not even move when dark clouds threaten
more rain. They will not move till she has sung her last
encore.*

*They wait for the woman who thirty years ago had
set out with Professor Thomas A. Dorsey to give America
songs that connected blacks' presence to the American
dream. "Gospel songs," she had said, "are the songs of
hope. Blues are the songs of despair." She remembered
that blacks sang in Africa to make the soil right for plant-
ing. They sang to make the harvest plentiful. They sang
when rotten slave ships brought them in chains across the
deep river the white man called the Atlantic Ocean. She
knew the sadness of those songs when the black man, even
after Emancipation, found himself still outside the American dream. He was free, the white man said—but not
quite free enough to vote, hold office, gain justice in a
court of law.*

*The sad songs passed from generation to generation.
And Mahalia had been listening to them almost from the
day she was born. By five she had begun singing them
herself, keeping them alive while she scrubbed and worked
the way the blacks had who made these songs. She didn't
let anyone tamper with their truth. She remembered God,
and God did not forget her. One of her favorite songs was
"I Believe." She did believe. Her faith was in every note
she sang.*

*The storm holds off a while. Mahalia stands up to
sing. She clasps her hands in front of her like a queen.*

She stands straight and tall. She looks above the crowd, sees the storm hovering over the heat. She closes her eyes. Bits of conversation drift up:

> *"Sister Haley's ready."*
> *"Ain't she beautiful!"*
> *"She's one of the anointed."*
> *"She's all together and well wrapped."*

Mahalia begins to sing "Just a Closer Walk with Thee." As she whispers the notes, she moves closer to the audience and they to her. She sings remembering Rosa Parks, remembering the Greensboro students, remembering how her people marched through snarling dogs, through tear gas and baseball bats wielded by goons. They marched in Birmingham, Hattiesburg, Chicago, Pittsburgh. They marched for the Civil Rights Act of 1957, for another piece of civil rights in 1960, for more civil rights in 1964. They marched. . . .

Mahalia's next song, "Take My Hand Precious Lord," had been Martin Luther King's favorite. Tears come to the eyes of many. Some weep openly for their murdered leader, a man of peace, who preached nonviolence and got shot in the head. And now they see tears streaming down Mahalia's cheeks. They cry for Medgar Evers, for President John F. Kennedy, for his brother, Robert. For Malcolm X, for Schwerner and Goodman and Chaney, the three young men murdered in Mississippi. For Mrs. Liuzzo, killed during the march on Birmingham. For Addie Mae Collins, Denise McNair, Carol Robertson, and Cynthia Wesley, children who died in a Birmingham Sunday

School one bright morning when dynamite ended hope.
For Mahalia's mother, Charity, and the slave ancestors she
lies next to on the plantation burial ground. . . .

"We want you to sing at our church benefit, Sister Haley," they'd say.

"The kids in our hospital need cheering. Won't you come?"

"Our cons would like to hear you," a warden would write her.

People were always asking Mahalia to do something. In 1971, when she was sixty, the government asked her to fly to an American outpost in Japan to sing for the soldiers. Mahalia's doctors had warned her against such trips. Since 1964 she had been in and out of hospitals, seriously ill again and again from heart trouble. She had to think hard about this request. Yes, she'd go. This last time.

How could she stop singing the Gospel? "I have hopes that my singing will break down some of the hate and fear that divide the white and black people," she said.

When she got back from Japan, they had another chore for her. It was to be Germany, this time. There was trouble between black and white American troops stationed there. Maybe Mahalia's golden voice and majestic presence would bring peace between them. That Thanksgiving of 1971 found her at an army post in Germany. She sang the old gospel songs with a special tenderness.

Then she collapsed on the stage and was rushed to an Army hospital, gravely ill. The doctors wanted to keep her there until she was strong enough to return to America. Mahalia shook her head. She thought she'd have a better chance of recovery back home. She did not want to die away from friends. If the end was coming, she wanted it to come in her own land.

They brought her back to Little Company of Mary Hospital in a Chicago suburb. And the newspapers told the story. "Sister Haley in a hospital," people said. This had happened often before. Even so, the hospital's switchboard was kept busy night and day as people called to find out how Sister Haley was doing. The President of the United States called. Letters poured in for the gospel queen. Flowers from friends and strangers banked her room. All this fuss over a down-home girl. Mahalia had been poor so long she never got used to a lot of attention.

On Thursday, January 27, 1972, Mahalia died. The news spread quickly through the city, and then across the nation. Many of her followers refused to believe it at first. When her pastor said her remains could be seen at Greater Salem Baptist Church, they came to see her for the last time. Fifty thousand citizens, black and white, came. In subzero weather they stood outside the church in a slow-moving line, waiting to pass Mahalia's body. Mean and shifty gales swept off frozen Lake Michigan, battering the mourners. But the cold could not discourage those who came to say goodbye.

The next day six thousand people came to Mahalia's funeral service. Aretha Franklin sang gospel songs that Mahalia had taught her.

Three days later, New Orleans was given a chance to pay its respects to Mahalia. The governor of Louisiana and the mayor of New Orleans led fifty thousand citizens in this final tribute. Then Mahalia was taken to her grave beside the Mississippi River, not far from Water Street.

She was home at last.

If you never hear me sing no more,
Aw, meet me on the other shore,
God's gonna separate the wheat from the tares,
Didn't he say.

Index

ABOUT THE AUTHOR

Jesse Jackson's enthusiasm for gospel music began when he was a small boy in Columbus, Ohio. He was fascinated by the songs he heard in the Baptist church there, and his continuing interest has led to this biography of the greatest of all gospel singers, Mahalia Jackson. Mr. Jackson is the author of many distinguished books for young readers. His first novel, *Call Me Charley*, was honored by the Child Study Association, and another of his novels, *Anchor Man*, won an award from the Council of Christians and Jews. Among his recent books are *The Sickest Don't Always Die the Quickest* and *The Fourteenth Cadillac*.

Mr. Jackson was born in Columbus, Ohio, and attended Ohio State University School of Journalism. He has lectured at Rutgers, St. John's, Ohio State, and Appalachian State universities, and frequently addresses teachers, librarians, and young readers in many parts of the country. During the spring of 1974 he served on the faculty of Appalachian State University. With his wife and daughter Judith he lives in New York City.